TONITE, TONITE

Cover design by Michael Trotman

About the Author

NEIL ARENA was a founder member of the acclaimed vocal group, the Mello-Kings. Singing baritone in the original five-piece version formed in 1956, he appeared on some of their best-loved recordings, including *Tonite, Tonite*, which still regularly appears in lists of the greatest doo wop songs of all time. Neil lives in Virginia, USA.

BEN STEPHENS is an author and journalist from London, UK. He writes about music, sport, business and politics.

www.benstephens.org

Tonite, Tonite

THE STORY OF THE ORIGINAL MELLO-KINGS

Neil Arena

Tonite, Tonite

ISBN: 9781739083199

To my mother, Gemma Albero Arena,
for teaching me to dream big and reach for the stars

Tonite, Tonite

Acknowledgements

This book had been formulating in my head for a very, very long time, possibly since not long after I left the Mello-Kings in 1958. Even though I was not yet a man and still living in the moment like most teenagers, I still knew right back then that I was very fortunate to be part of something so special.

I am indebted to the many friends and colleagues who helped me put my story on paper in the last two years. Special thanks are owed, however, to:

Rosemarie Denison Arena, Larry Esposito, Marjorie Baird,
Mary Ann Gassmann, Vickie Gassmann, Allen Spath,
Cal Lynch, Robert Di Fiore, Larry Chance, David Fordham,
Michael Trotman, Neal Basson, Ellen Silver Stange,
Sarah Smith. Melissa Owusu and the Belmont Country Club.

Without you this tale might never have been told.

N.A. November 2022

'There are no tickets left… It would have been an all-star line-up: Chuck Berry, the Mello-Kings, Gloria Hofstadt and me!'

Potsie Weber, Happy Days
S1 E05 Hardware Jungle

‘The music of your youth stays with you throughout your life’

Dick Clark

Contents

Prologue

THE teacher didn't look like the kind of guy you'd mess with. He wasn't young, certainly in his sixties, but still heavy set with a broken nose. The bow tie did nothing to diminish his menacing demeanour.

John Caville looked a little like William Bendix. The nose had been smashed in a car accident many years earlier and he delighted in pressing it flat during class to freak out the kids. Mr Caville taught office machines and business law to 11th and 12th grade high school students. He was tough if you fooled around, but here was I getting up and walking out in the middle of class.

"Neil, where are you going?"

"Mr Caville, we have a one week gig at the Apollo. I need to get going for a train to Grand Central Station then on to Harlem."

I was lucky: the big man liked me and had always come to all my basketball games at school; he was used to me being something of a wise guy and knew that I was more than capable of acing his class and all the tests. We'd usually figure something out to square my poor attendance, but this time had I gone too far?

JOHN M. CAVILLE

Wondering himself if my last chance had already passed, Mr Caville was lost for words. To be fair, there wasn't a lot he could say that would make any kid or teacher think it made sense to swap being a 16 year old rock and roll star for the joys of a Burroughs adding machine.

Eventually, referring to rock and roll's pioneering but controversial DJ of the time, Mr Caville said: "Neil, you know, Alan Freed is a son only a mother could love."

Snickering from my friends in class.

He continued: "Are you going to be here for the test tomorrow?"

"Sir, we have a matinee tomorrow."

He unnarrowed his eyes and then rolled them. Opening his notebook, he told me he was marking a zero against my name for the next day's test.

For me, it was no big deal. It had gotten to the point where I was only attending half of Mr Caville's classes and my grades yo-yoed between a zero for a test I didn't sit or a great mark for when I bothered to show up.

I kept walking and never looked back.

Chapter 1

Mount Vernon's Got Talent

THE path from an Italian American working class family in New York to the stage and recording studio is well trodden. Did I plan that journey for myself? Not at all. It just happened. Growing up in the early 1950s I was obviously aware of countless showbusiness successes with roots in the 'old country': Julius La Rosa, Jimmy Durante, Frankie Laine, Jimmy Rosselli and, of course, the great Mario Lanza all loomed large among my earliest musical memories. They were followed by global superstars such as Frank Sinatra, Tony Bennett and my own hero in those days, Dean Martin. Well into the 21st century, Italian musical genes are still never far from the Billboard charts or Madison Square Garden – Madonna, Jon Bon Jovi, Lady Gaga and many more.

Needless to say, many of these stars had changed or at least adapted their birthnames ahead of hitting the big time. To give you one example from my youth, Vic Damone was born Vito Rocco Farinola in Brooklyn, NY.

I came into the world as Aniello Guerino Arena on 9 May 1940. My family lived in Mount Vernon, a city of only four square miles in southern Westchester County, NY, around 17 miles northeast of

Manhattan and just above the Bronx. Mount Vernon was, and still is, a very multicultural place in line with many other cities in New York state where immigrants from Europe had settled and quickly put down roots. Everyone seemed to get along pretty well and the small, hardworking city seems to have produced a huge number of successful people during my lifetime. They include actors Art Carney, Denzel Washington and Sidney Poitier; musicians Sean "P. Diddy" Combs and Heavy D; two-time world heavyweight boxing champion Floyd Patterson; and the man who changed the way Americans listened to pop music – Dick Clark.

My parents were both Italian, although my dad, Augustino (Augie), had been born in Brazil, to which his own father had emigrated from Sarno, just inland from the Bay of Naples, behind Pompeii. My mom, Gemma, had a much larger family from Sicily and they had a greater involvement in my life. I was the eldest of three kids: I have a sister Marie and a 'baby' brother William, 15 years younger, who sadly died after a heart attack, aged 56, in 2011.

Our home at 131 South 12th Avenue 10550 was a relatively modest house on three floors, including the basement. It's still there 80 years later, unrecognizable after probably several refurbishments, in a street that looks upscale of how we lived then. Even so, we had more than enough space. Marie and I each had a bedroom; my maternal grandparents lived in rooms on the left side of the first floor, my parents on the right side. Best of all, there was a 'dumb waiter' for carrying stuff up and down between floors. You don't have to ask: of course I used to ride in it!

Gabriel Albero, my grandfather, remains to this day the greatest influence on my life and was certainly my first exposure to music. Neither he nor his wife, Lucy, spoke any English, but this was no barrier to living a full and fun life - at least for him – in the autumn of their years. Gabriel was a real character; a boozer and a womanizer. He made wine in the cellar: a rough, Italian-style red;

a fake Chianti that I was more than happy to help him concoct and test out.

But it was upstairs on the porch that I would sing with Gabriel, honing my young voice on the old Italian songs. The old rascal would take me and his crooning to the beach at New Rochelle where, on Sunday afternoons, the Italian ladies would hang out in groups. He would find a way of sparking a conversation with them (I can't be sure to what extent they understood his Sicilian dialect) and before too long he'd be singing *C'è la luna mezzo mare*, affecting tears and drying his eyes at the end. That song was later sung by Mamma Corleone and an old guy in the wedding scene of The Godfather movie. If Francis Ford Coppola had come from New Rochelle, instead of Detroit, I might have speculated that he'd spotted us in his childhood. Anyway, we must have cut a comical picture, the shameless old warbler and his grandson, as we promenaded through Glen Island in search of a captive audience. In hindsight, it may have been Gabriel's primary way of communicating.

******

If Gabriel was a happy drinker, my dad Augie was the polar opposite; I'll get back to that later. For now, suffice it to say that he wasn't a noticeably happy man in any way, despite having a great deal to be happy about, at least until my young adult years: a great wife, fairly relaxed in-laws and beautiful, talented kids. He also had his own little business, a shoe shop just round the corner from home. Dad was the first person to buy shoes from outside suppliers and sell them in his own independent store, alongside a busy shoe repair counter. Customers would travel a long way to get their shoes mended there, to a very high standard. When the store originally opened in New Rochelle, before Dad moved it to Mount Vernon,

Yankees star and Baseball Hall of Famer Lou Gehrig was a loyal customer. Dad also had a concession, within the store, for the 3D Dry Cleaning Company in Eastchester. In my later teens, if he was busy waiting for a shoe delivery, I would bag up the dry cleaning and drive it to 3D. In some ways, Dad was quite the entrepreneur.

On an emotional level, however, he was a car crash. A difficult man not given to showing affection, Dad rarely praised me and certainly never said anything loving to my face, but when the hit records came my picture was pasted all over the walls of the shop. "That's my son!" he'd be sure to tell customers, who'd heard it many times before. Until then, although he followed my efforts across a wide range of sports with great interest, he was usually critical, focusing on the minor elements that hadn't quite been pulled off, rather than major achievements and results.

Gemma Albero Arena, by contrast, was hugely affectionate and much more demonstrative. I couldn't have wished for a better mother. She had my back at all times, was extremely supportive and just 'got it' when it came to maintaining a happy family in reasonably challenging circumstances. Her own childhood had been stable and loving; it's no surprise that I became very close to my grandparents. Mom was devoted to us and worked tirelessly, both at home and outside, to keep things happy and on track. It was about keeping the peace, more than anything else. In truth, it was about managing Dad's moods and his temper.

It's a surprise Mom got so much done, since she was very scatty. Looking at it another way, she had so much to juggle that it's amazing she didn't drop balls all the time. Mom had a job at Jaffe's Candy Factory, just a couple of blocks away. Despite the proximity of her work, she was often late to show up because she would lose track of time. Organization and multitasking were not her strong suits. Even so, she was loved by the Jaffe family who owned the business and she never got close to being fired. This was a blessing because her financial contribution to our home would later turn out to be more critical than originally planned. Her secure position at Jaffe's also gave her the flexibility to continue waiting on Dad, hand and foot, when needed.

Mom may have taken her eye of the ball with housework from time to time, but she never stopped cooking. Sometimes she cooked all day long, as if for a special occasion, but that was the effort required to keep Dad fed and well-behaved. However tight money eventually became, Dad always ate like a millionaire: T-bone steaks; rabbit, perhaps in a cacciatore or braised with rosemary; and my own favorite, traditional Italian meatballs, made with ground beef and sausage, mixed with breadcrumbs and parsley. The ungrateful sonofabitch often had these wonderful delicacies hand-delivered to his store by Mom and, years later, by me. When we were eating at home as a family, if the food wasn't to his liking he'd erupt like the Vesuvio of his ancestors and turn the table upside down in a rage.

******

Starting school gave me a bigger stage on which to perform in every sense, not just singing, which until then had been confined to the stoop at home. At five years old I was sent to a preschool. Our Lady of Mount Carmel, located 50 yards from the Catholic church of the same name on South 10th Avenue, was a small but austere institution run by nuns. As a first rung on the academic ladder it was a great route to discouraging a child from progressing in education. While I'm sure the teaching methods favored by these mainly old ladies were broadly effective for imparting basic reading, writing and arithmetic skills in readiness for elementary school, the sometimes brutal approach made me hate every minute spent within those miserable walls. One evil teacher, the old and lanky Sister Teresa, beat me more than once for nothing in particular. I can still see her cold, grey, skinny face peering at me from beneath her veil and coif as she leaned in towards a cowering child whose feet didn't even reach the floor when seated at his little desk.

The desk was the issue. An individual wooden chest on legs, with slanted surface and inkwell in the corner, I would keep my lunch inside, among the few books that were needed at that very young age. One day, when lunchtime arrived, I just wasn't hungry. Actually I was feeling a little nauseous at the thought of my mother's tuna sandwiches, which were a little oily for my taste.

"Where's your lunch, Neil?"

"I ate it."

"No you didn't – open up your desk."

I looked at her, knowing I'd been backed into a corner because she'd caught me lying.

"Don't you know it's a sin to waste food?"

"I'm just not hungry, Sister."

I lifted the splintery wooden lid of the desk with dread and was forced to eat my unappetizing lunch, but not before my misdemeanor had provoked predictably disproportionate anger from my penguin-like tormentor.

My perceived insolence was met with a swift whack to the hand with a long wooden ruler, followed by the tears I couldn't suppress by clenching my quivering lips. Looking back, it amazes me that however decrepit and elderly some teachers were in those days, not just nuns, they were able to summon the reflexes and athleticism of Zorro when they wanted to dish out corporal punishment with whatever weapon came to hand. That said, a five year old hand just isn't cut out for that sort of abuse, and I've never pretended that such brutal forms of discipline have made me the fine, upstanding man I am. In any event, after running away several times from that hellhole during the single month I was there, Mom eventually withdrew me.

******

Not long after, I was able to join first grade at Grimes Elementary School, between South 10th and 11th Avenues, and only two blocks from home. A much larger, double fronted affair with a 1930s façade, this finally felt like what I had imagined school to be – I had never not wanted to go to school; it had just been a bad start. My formative years got into full swing at Grimes. Before long, I was trying, and beginning to excel at, all kinds of sports and games. I was slower to get going with reading, but my 3rd grade teacher, Miss Sposato, was patient and helpful, deciding that holding me

Grimes Elementary School, Mount Vernon

down a year at that early stage would work out best in the long run. She was right. I made steady, unspectacular progress in my early academics, while continuing to develop as a great little all-rounder at sport, not least in baseball and basketball. Years later I would have Miss Sposato's sister as my Home Room teacher. They both became happy memories of my school years.

My only disappointment at Grimes was the lack of an actual basketball team to join. All my playing was done out of school, although many hours were spent refining my skills in its playground, sometimes until late. Still relatively small of stature, I would spin the ball off the fence and into a barrel, where eventually the ball would be hidden until I returned to play again. Across the street from the playground was a gas station, run by a friendly young guy called Gary. Short, but wiry and strong, Gary was clearly a sports fan and showed great interest in my practice sessions. One late afternoon, he walked over.

"If I move one of my spotlights on top of the garage, would that help you shoot for longer at night?" offered Gary.

I would be indebted to Gary for the rest of my basketball career. More practice got me picked for Jimmy Ritz's local team and it wasn't too many years before I scored 33 points - in the days before three point field goals – which became the highest in the county. My team's total was 53.

My academic prowess made a leap forward between 7th and 8th grade. I had a champion and great supporter in Miss Lyons, an 'old maid' spinster with permanently pursed lips on a rugged face who would make the kids repeat work until they got it right. You can't argue with 'practice makes perfect', an approach that later underpinned the punishing rehearsal schedule of the Mello-Kings. Miss Lyons had a good friend of a similar vintage, Miss Twist, who taught algebra. Porcelain-skinned and auburn-haired, old Miss Twist had a nervous habit of repeatedly smoothing down her dress with her hand. It's a wonder it wasn't shiny on one side. Nonetheless, she was a great math teacher and, with her guidance, the penny suddenly dropped for me and within a few months I went from a relative dum-dum 7th grader to a star 8th grader.

My star was in the ascendant, so Miss Lyons was disappointed when I said I wasn't running for school President. I had already agreed to be campaign manager for Abe Middleton, a bright and popular black kid who had become a great friend.

NEIL ARENA, Con Edison Sports Award winner, shows the medallion to his grandfather, Gabriel Albero, who retired from the company's Westchester C & M Bureau in 1957. Neil was honored for skill in basketball at A.B. Davis High School, the 277th student to win the award in the past six years.

"Are you sure you don't want to run?" she said, "I don't know why; I think you'd have a good chance and would make a great President."

"No Miss, I've made notes and I'm going to introduce Abe on the dais."

Determined to help me shine in some way, Miss Lyons rehearsed me and taught me my first valuable lessons in public speaking which, within a small number of years, I would use on a much bigger stage to introduce the group. The election gave me a small introduction to the spotlight, Abe won by a landslide and Miss Lyons was very proud of both of us.

More than a decade later, double Oscar winner and former Mount Vernon resident Denzel Washington would be the star turn at Grimes. But before he had even joined the school, I took my ball skills and increasingly confident singing voice several blocks east to Washington Junior High on South 5th Avenue.

******

I can't remember any academic aspect of my time at Washington, but again I was blessed with a teacher, this time in 9th grade, who was on my side and wouldn't let my laziness get the better of me. Mrs. Utley was my home room teacher. She was in her thirties, heavy-set with fair skin and red hair. Her husband taught science at the same school. She could tell I was essentially a bright kid who needed cajoling to stick with the program and come out the other side ready for High School. Establishing a contract of trust and mutual respect between us, Mrs. Utley basically *made* me come to school every day and on time, an effort which required me to run almost six blocks in the morning to keep our agreement. Why did I do it for her? I think I was very cognizant of my limitations when it came to self-discipline. I knew even at the beginning of my teens that I needed some form of mentor or manager at all times to keep me moving forward during that period. That was never going to come from home. My potential talents in studies, sports and music may have been matched by energy and ambition, but not by drive.

Mrs. Utley was keen for my mom and dad to come to one of the parents' evenings at the school. Perhaps she thought they might better understand what could be possible if my potential was harnessed and encouraged. Wishful thinking on her part. My parents never went to anything, let alone a school event. In fact they rarely left the house together. Anyways, it would have involved Mom taking half a day to get ready.

"If it's about babysitting, I'll look after your little brother," Mrs. Utley insisted. So that's what happened. She did indeed come to the house to make my parents' attendance possible.

It was at Washington Junior High that my singing career began in earnest. As soon as people knew that I had the makings of a good voice, I quickly became the teachers' lazy go-to option for providing entertainment in school assemblies. Sometimes my singing had no relevance whatsoever to the day's proceedings or theme; I was simply a musical interlude among the boring school notices, warnings and updates. Scheduled to sing only one song, my couple of minutes in front of the school invariably stretched to a short set of popular romantic songs normally delivered by someone much older. *Because of You* was always a good opener, often followed by *Rags to Riches, Your Cheatin' Heart* and the particularly sickly *Vaya Con Dios.*

"He's got a wonderful voice, but why does he sing those mushy love songs?" I overheard one lady say above the enthusiastic applause.

It seems a reasonable question now, but what was I supposed to sing if not ballads? It was 1952-53. Rock and roll hadn't yet been invented. Nobody had thought to fuse three-chord blues with swing to change the face of popular music forever; the teenager hadn't yet arrived. My only points of reference were balladeers: early Sinatra, Tony Bennett, Dean Martin. They were to remain my inspiration all the way through the teen idol doo-wop years and beyond.

It was back in 5th grade that my singing ability had first been noticed. Discovered may be an exaggeration, because it was a surprise to me when my school music teacher, Miss Corocoran, said to me: "You have a voice – and I don't think you know it."

"I don't know what you're talking about, Miss," I replied and gave it no further consideration. My love of singing continued to grow steadily without me even noticing and by 12 I was singing in Little League dinners. I played ball with a kid called Freddie Cassucci. His mom played the piano and encouraged me to perform at these events, where she would accompany me. Dressed in suit and tie, crowned with Vaseline Hair Tonic, I would deliver crowd pleasers such as Frankie Laine's *I Believe*. I still sing that song to anyone who cares to listen; I also stuck with the Vaseline tonic and 70 years later I have a very decent head of hair. Just saying.

******

I was a regular at talent shows in the Westchester area. They were small events, just for fun, but it wasn't unusual for music managers and talent spotters – some of whom ran their own radio shows and concerts - to trawl around these places in the long-shot hope of making a bankable new discovery. That was how two well-dressed guys in their thirties and holding briefcases came to be knocking on my parents' front door one evening.

"Your son has a great deal of talent, Mr. Arena. You must be very proud." The more experienced and possibly senior of the two agents chose an unoriginal opening shot for this discussion that I, watching from the sidelines, knew was doomed from the start. My mom viewed quietly from the kitchen table as the showbiz guys talked to The Boss, as my dad liked family and friends to call him.

"Why don't you sing something for us, Neil?" the second agent said.

I dutifully, if predictably, broke into *Because of You*. When I'd finished, the two guys looked at each other, nodding with satisfaction. They turned to Mom, to check her mood and how she might react to their next move; then they turned to Dad while opening a briefcase to pull out a document.

"Mr. Arena, we have a contract here for you. We'd be very excited to work with Neil, so -"

"No, no, no, no, no! I'm not having my son sign anything. I don't want you owning him. You can leave it there, but we won't be signing."

Dad wasn't necessarily wrong. Many agents had a reputation for exploiting young talent for their own gain and never sharing the spoils fairly; sometimes not at all. As Hunter S Thompson said 20 years later, "The music business is a cruel and shallow money trench, a long plastic hallway where thieves and pimps run free." We never discussed the contract again, but I continued to take part in talent shows and singing carried on growing as an important part of my young life.

******

Apart from the hits of Frankie Laine, Johnny Desmond and Hank Williams, numbers from the golden era of musicals in the 1940s and early 1950s were also, unsurprisingly, a big feature of any singer's repertoire at that time. Rogers and Hammerstein seemed unbeatable and the WJH production of South Pacific turned out to be an important platform for me. It was also how I met the guy who would change my life: Dick Levister.

Everyone in Mount Vernon who had any interest in music knew Richard 'Dick' Levister. He was the leader of the King Levister Orchestra but worked chiefly as a musical director and was in huge demand from schools, colleges and showbiz agents. As a black, gay guy, Dick wasn't easily forgotten. Outwardly conservative in appearance, always in a sport coat and necktie, he was thin and well-groomed. Strangely, his gravelly voice couldn't sing a note, despite the inestimable musical talent he could draw on. In a time when homosexual men were considered an oddity at best, there was nothing overtly gay about Dick – although his sexuality was no big secret. The greatest clue was possibly the company he kept around town, not least a couple of particularly flamboyant local characters, Charlie Pom-Pom and Rico.

South Pacific at WJH would turn out to be the 'Big Bang' moment that set in motion the creation and evolution of the Mello-Kings. I was the only one my future co-singers to attend WJH. My teachers and Dick had already picked me, based on my record of performing at school events, to showcase my voice in the show with an initially solo segment in which I would sing "I Am the Song'; this was followed by another boy, responding with "I Am the Dance". How this came to fit in with the rest of South Pacific, I can't pretend to remember, but I would have been sure to milk the part for all it was worth.

Bobby Scholl, his brother Jerry and their friend Eddie Quinn auditioned after seeing a newspaper advertisement looking to fill places in the South Pacific chorus. The wannabe singers joined as 'sailors', and I didn't have a great deal to do with them. We all had a good time and after the show finished it would be perhaps another year before I saw those guys again.

Chapter 2

The Battle of Turn Hall

A.B. Davis High School was known as 'the synagogue on the hill'. Let me explain: we estimated at the time that around 80% of the students were Jewish. No more than 10% would have been Italian-American, like me, with the rest a mix of kids descended from Irish, Polish or German immigrants, as well as a few from longer settled families of English, Scottish or Scandinavian provenance.

The 'hill' was the tallest in the city of Mount Vernon and had once been called Chester Hill, now in the Chester Heights district. Former state senator and Mount Vernon resident Ruth Hassell-Thompson, who had a brother and a sister at Davis in the years either side of my time there, has said the school's students were proud, bordering on snobby about their hilltop place of learning; it was viewed as far superior to Edison Tech, the largely vocational school that accommodated the mostly Italian and black students living in the cold-water flats on the south end of town. The two schools eventually merged in 1964.

S 12th Street wasn't far south, but I still lived closer to Edison. However, I really wasn't technically inclined and I wanted to go to Davis – and Irv Halstead wanted me to go there too. Irv was head of basketball and baseball there. Edison's coach, John Branca, had wanted me too and he knew talent, since he was the brother of Ralph 'Hawk' Branca, the star pitcher who played 12 seasons of Major League Baseball for the Brooklyn Dodgers, Detroit Tigers and New York Yankees. Ironically, Hawk had also graduated from Davis before briefly attending NYU. I became the only Italian kid on the basketball team. There were no black players, either. I had played against some of the others while in at WJH – Jimmy Gross, Mark Klein, Jerry Fuchs and Jim Snyder and they'd all been looking forward to being on the same team as me when they learned I was joining Davis.

The main school building seemed immense. An incredibly wide 1930s building, slightly austere, with three floors and a basement. Either side of the central entrance, with its grand steps and columns, were at least 20 windows on each floor. These days it wouldn't look out of place as a very large, out-of-town corporate headquarters. For all the messing about and fun we had during our schooldays, the place looked very serious and carried with it a distinct sense of foreboding. Showing up for the first time as a 15 year old and mounting those steps was pretty scary; it was scarier a couple years later when I slipped on what I thought was the first step, but was in fact a sheet of ice. I was lucky to escape with only a sore ass. I only knew one or two people already at Davis or joining at the same time. Ray Motta had been a friend for some years and was a junior, a year ahead of me. Ray lived in the Bronx, so strictly speaking wasn't in the right district for Davis, but he had registered under the address of his cousin Freddie Corrado.

Mount Vernon High School, Mt. Vernon, N. Y.
221302

A.B.Davis, later Mount Vernon High School

Ray's father owned a fish market and was reasonably successful. We would play basketball in the Mottas' backyard and enjoy hanging out together. Anyone watching us play would have laughed at the spectacle of 5'7" Neil stealing the ball from 6'4" Ray, but what I found the funniest about our height difference was how my opponent seemed to eat far less than me. Ray would take a small sandwich from his lunchbox at school, while I would leave home with a huge feast prepared by my mother. Perhaps Ray's appetite had been dulled by the packs of cigarettes he would keep tucked under the sleeves of his T shirt, a 'cool' look he had adopted that was completed by an impressive pair of Elvis sideburns. Despite all our yard practice, Ray never made the team: in school training he was regularly called out for 'traveling' - taking too many steps without dribbling the ball.

The first teacher to make an impression on me in the earlier days at Davis was Ezeka Jewell, who taught biology. A very tall man in his 40s with a small head on top of wide shoulders, Mr Jewell came to every home game I played. He was there when the magnificently named Dashaway Hadaway from the White Plains High School team stepped on my toe and injured my ankle, which Mr Jewell bandaged. I missed four games after that. Back in class, Mr Jewell's custom was to eat his lunch while teaching. Possibly attempting to make his own mastication relevant to the lesson, he would always look at the class and say: "You have to chew your food well." I can't remember if this pearl of wisdom then led to a biological discussion about digestion or enzymes, but it wouldn't have helped me much: I eventually had to quit the class because it didn't fit in with my sporting and, later, musical schedule. It was the same in math: after excelling in algebra at WJH, I took geometry at Davis to support my ultimate intention of going to college and playing basketball; again my lessons fell by the wayside as I spent more time making music than doing homework. My report card was so red with 'incompletes' that it looked more like a Christmas card. My mom signed it anyway; she wanted me to follow my dreams. My fellow students were also supportive. On my way to quitting biology I found an unlikely ally in the shape of Gerry Blank, a studious and uncontroversial girl who, I seem to remember, eventually became a teacher herself. Gerry would slide the answers towards me whenever we had a test; it was a very kind gesture which was hugely appreciated, but my move to another biology class to fit my own schedule meant that I lost her help.

In my sophomore year, I started dating my high school sweeetheart, Mary Ann Lieto. It began in the same way I suppose teenagers meet now. One of her friends came up to me at school and told me Mary Ann liked me, then thrust her number into my hand. I was aware of Mary Ann from my biology class, but hadn't really given her much thought until then. We sat in order of last name, so I was positioned at the front, from which I used to turn and scope the class for chicks. Mary Ann and Sheila Lidsky were two beauties: Sheila became a cheerleader; many years later I would visit her in Philadelphia.

My reaction to Mary Ann's reported interest was kind of "well, if she likes me, what the hell!". I quickly realized there was a lot to like about her, not just her long brown hair, great figure and beautiful smile. She wasn't yet old enough to be compared to a movie star of that era, but over the years I've looked back and remembered her resembling a young Julia Roberts. Not too shabby! Our first date was, predictably, at the movies. We headed to the RKO Proctor's Theater on Gramatan Avenue, more often than not to catch a Jerry Lewis movie, and sat in the balcony, as most lovers did. From that early age, I always kept my dates on my left. I found it was easier for me to turn in that direction when going in for the kiss.

Mary Ann and I dated for three years, including the inevitable break periods that kids still have when they're going steady. She caught me misbehaving twice. The first time happened when I was waiting around to meet a girl who was well known at school for being free with her favors. I had arranged an 'appointment', only to be told by the girl at the last minute that she was otherwise engaged. Unfortunately Mary Ann happened to swing by while this disappointing information was being communicated, which earned me a well-deserved slap. The second time, also in my senior year, was when she learned I had been unfaithful with a lovely girl called Judy Ganeles. Apparently, Judy was supposed to be off school and sick at home, but she and I still arranged to meet at her place. Judy had the most stunning green eyes; truly mesmerising. We reconnected briefly (and unromantically) after I'd left both the Mello-Kings and Davis. Judy's father worked in the Brill Building, the famous hit song factory. I had made a solo recording, funded to the tune of $500 by a generous theater angel, Gerald Rosenberg, whom I'd known while caddying at the Metropolis Country Club in White Plains. It was an perfectly good, if unremarkable, version of *The Second Time Around,* the Sammy Cahn / Jimmy van Heusen song originally recorded by Bing Crosby and then Frank Sinatra. I took it over to Judy's for her dad to listen to, but after knowing me for doo-wop and R&B, her reaction was along the lines of: "Neil, what *is* this? What happened to those great songs you used to sing on stage?". Yep, my true musical tastes hadn't been changed by a spell as a teen idol.

******

Alan Pilson was a Davis friend who'd also been with me at Washington Junior High. He was a frustrated singer: not blessed with an amazing voice, but he loved rock and roll, and singing *a capella* in the hallways at school. Alan had a great sense of humor, as well as being very smart and an excellent student. We became big buddies and, although our paths diverged dramatically after school, we tried to stay in touch. Whenever there was a school reunion in the decades that followed, Alan would make sure we sang together and it was always the same number: not a favourite from our teenage years, but the 1962 hit by Don and Juan, *What's Your Name*. I was sad to hear of Alan's passing in 2016, but honored to have been mentioned in his New York Times obituary. My schoolfriend had become a very successful copyright lawyer, yet continued to entertain friends and colleagues with impromptu doo wop serenades while dining in some of Manhattan's finest restaurants. He was quite a guy.

Frank Piccinini was a very different singing buddy from school. His family lived in Mount Vernon and I was also friendly with his sister and parents. It was Frank who first alerted me to the opportunity of my life.

"The Mellotones are auditioning for a baritone," he told me excitedly as we hung around in the hallway at Davis.

"How do you know?"

"I ran into Levister. They'll be at Larry Esposito's house on Saturday night. I'm going."

Larry was a slightly older guy, out of his teens, whom Levister had put together with South Pacific extras the Scholl brothers and Eddie Quinn to form a vocal group.

We went together. Larry lived on Columbus Avenue and had a piano, which he played pretty well by ear. These sorts of gatherings in the homes of would-be musicians were happening all over the New York area at that time. Everybody wanted to be a recording artist, or part of a group, at any rate.

Frank went before me. He had to jump in on *Honey Honey* by Frankie Lymon and the Teenagers, and then their bigger hit, *Why Do Fools Fall In Love?* Frank did great, but they liked me more. He later said it could never have worked out for him because his folks wouldn't have let him go on tour. As I repeated the two songs, the other guys looked at each other and smiled as we all bounced harmonies off each other. They knew they had found their baritone and so did Levister. The man knew music.

"Come to the Boys' Club on Monday for rehearsals. You're in."

******

My first gig with the fledgling Mellotones was the following Saturday night at the Standard AC at the Bronx end of Mount Vernon's Sandford Boulevard, not far from the Boys' Club. The AC was kind of a private club, although that's possibly a generous description. It was like a house with a bar and a piano, and it could hold about 100 people. Performers starting out would play there to a mildly interested clientele and payment was on a pass-the-hat basis. Joe Bruni, a slightly older guy we knew who was no longer at school, had recommended us and that night very kindly set the hat on its way by putting in $5 – quite a lot at that time. Bruni's buddy, one of the men running the club, came to fetch us from outside.

"Tonight we're presenting the Mellotones," he announced without too much ceremony, once he had decided enough people would hear him above the chatter. The hat was passed round without too much enthusiasm.

"Come on guys, the Mellotones aren't going to play for nothing. Make it right for them to be here!"

As the almost exclusively male crowd reluctantly dipped into their pockets, they could have been forgiven for thinking they were about to waste a couple of bucks on five kids in jeans accompanied by an older dude on a piano. By the end of our set – at least 10 songs from our list of current ballads – they were shouting for more. We came away with a very handsome $50 each and that was the night everybody started talking about us.

The money didn't stay in our own pockets for long because after that first gig we all knew we needed outfits for performing. Guided by the imagination and sophistication that you would expect from five boys with an average age of 17, we opted for white jackets paired with black pants (easy to keep clean), but white bucks as contrasting shoes. We figured that black shiny stage shoes would be too easily scuffed; white bucks with press-on straps would be quick to change into and could be cleaned with white polish. The logos on the jackets, which we sourced from a tuxedo and wedding shop in Mount Vernon, didn't come until later.

We couldn't wait to debut our new stage wardrobe, although the venue possibly didn't do it justice. We took a big pay cut to play Tucci's Bar and Grill in the Bronx, where we were given $10 each and free pizza. The Tucci family was well known in Mount Vernon and I'd grown up with a number of them. Their bar was very popular bar with a diverse crowd, from young couples to wise guys and chancers plus, of course, a regular flow of gay and transvestite customers. There was even an area towards the back of the premises that was effectively a gay hangout. That's where Levister's friend Rico could usually be found. Rico worked as a menswear salesman in a department store. I happened to spy him while I was shopping one day and cheerily called his name to say 'hi'.

"Do me a favor: don't call me Rico in the store," he urged, with a serious expression that really didn't suit him.

I'd assumed that Rico was his real name, but perhaps it was his *alter ego* while in Tucci's and similar establishments. I never did discover his real name, but suspected it might have been less 'exotic' and more in line with his daytime appearance: very small – at most 5'4" – yet a little dumpy and not particularly effeminate in his manner or gait; he wasn't light on his loafers. Levister's other friend from Tucci's, 'Charlie Pom Pom' (you guessed: not his real name either) was taller, by a whole foot, perhaps. Heavy set, too. The physical features of these two dudes made their transformation into dames even more remarkable. I was fooled, anyway, the first time I met saw them in the bar. Not permitted to drink at our young age, the best we could to do to look cool while sipping a soda in Tucci's before performing was to eye up the girls in a not-too-subtle way, promising a chance to hang with would-be pop stars.

"Look at those beautiful chicks over there," I said, leaning towards Eddie.

"Are you shitting me? said Eddie – they're in drag!! Ha haaaaaaa!!!" That raspy laugh was one of the highlights of every day Eddie and I spent together. The attention to detail by some of the Tucci's cross-dressers was very impressive: a variety of wigs in different colours, fancy dresses, stockings and suspenders, ladies' shoes in men's sizes; no two guys had arrived looking remotely similar. It was quite a parade.

We played almost exactly the same set as at the Standard AC, about 10 numbers; Levister hunched over the piano in his trademark poor posture, possibly a result of spending most of his waking hours at the keyboard. Right from the earliest days of the Mellotones, as we still were, Levister gave us enormous confidence in our performance because he had rehearsed us to perfection before every gig. He would tune each of our voices, one note one finger, and built all our harmonies - some of them very intricate – from the bottom up. Our unique takes on well-known ballads would, more often than not, blow the audience away, especially when we sang *a capella*. In later years, friends would tell me proudly that they used to look in on us from the hallway as we practised in our room at the boys club.

Friday night was pizza night in bars and eateries all over New York state in the Fifties. The tradition provided ready-made audiences for us when we were getting started. Customers from Tucci's recommended us to the owner of the Racine Way, a bar and club nearby in the Bronx, that later moved to the Saw Mill River Parkway. He came to see us and then booked us. The deal was the same: $10 each, but no sign of any pizza. After we played there every weekend for a month, I finally came to the conclusion that he was starting to rip us off.

"Guys, this is bullshit," I moaned to the others. "He needs to start paying us proper money."

As we got ready to leave at the end of the fourth Friday night, the owner said, "Great job guys, I'll be in touch to book you again. I walked up to him and said, "Sure but you need to pay more." There was no resistance; he knew he'd been exploiting a group of talented teenagers and that he'd still be on to a good thing if he gave us a raise.

"OK, OK, I'll pay $20 each," he said, without blinking. We went home feeling we'd won – after all, we'd doubled our money at a stroke – but it was still shit pay and there was still no pizza.

******

"Oop, oop! It's your man Coop!" was the cry of an energetic and ambitious DJ in New Rochelle called Cooper. Operating from a second floor studio over a bunch of stores on North Avenue, Cooper became well connected in an affluent area where many sports and media stars lived at the time. He graduated to putting on a big live show every month and got us to play a number of times before we started making records. We were booked as headliners at the Turn Hall in Mount Vernon, a sombre looking old building on 10th Avenue with spooky creepers growing all over it. The last time I had been there was for my Aunt Yolanda's wedding. Supporting us were two blondes from New Rochelle wearing white dresses, and Frankie Lymon's brother, Lewis, who appeared to be suffering from a sore throat; this required him to keep applying a strange orange powder that he produced from a bag at regular intervals with dipped wet fingers.

If it already sounds like a weird night, believe me, it was. Within a few minutes of the two blondes opening the show, a huge fight broke out in the packed hall. Most of the crowd was too young to drink, but everyone seemed to be on Seagram 7&7s. Before too long, drunken kids were flinging glasses at the stage and one of the blondes started bleeding from a cut. Frank Piccinini and Mary Ann had both come to watch us that night. He grabbed her and took her someplace safe, while we escaped out of the side door from the performers' end of the hall. The cops were called and arrived in six cars. They ejected the drunken hoodlums, restored order and eventually dispersed the wild crowd; but our evening, and many

Turn Hall, Mount Vernon

others', had been cut short by somebody's drink getting knocked over, or an accidental nudge of the wrong guy when walking past.

Before the chaos had begun, we were backstage getting introduced to a distinguished musical visitor. Jimmy Jones was a major figure on the New York doo wop scene. He was lead singer of The Pretenders in the mid-Fifties, as well as leading other vocal groups and penning several great songs for himself. His 1960 hit *Handy Man* would later become a favourite in folk-rock legend James Taylor's repertoire, while his lasting contribution to pop music until the present day was pioneering the falsetto vocal style in R&B. Jimmy was a very sweet, decent guy approaching his late 20s. Well dressed and relaxed, he stood out among the teenagers in Turn Hall. It was a shame he didn't get to see our set because we would have been right up his street; as a vocal perfectionist himself, he'd have enjoyed our attention to detail. Even so, meeting a star like Jimmy at that abortive gig in the middle of nowhere was one of the first times I began to realise that our group had a real chance of making it.

Happily, we remained firmly on Jimmy's radar from that point and ran into him many times, not just in the early days but also as recording stars. He was smiling at us from the front row of the Apollo, nodding to me while looking pleased that we'd begun to taste success. On another, less career-defining night, we hung out with Jimmy at the Fort Hill Dance Club in Yonkers, where the Cadillacs were performing. Who didn't love the Cadillacs? In many ways they started the fashion for slick, choreographed R&B groups that lasted right through the Sixties and Seventies. Their song *Speedoo* had been a massive hit the year before and the five of us were thrilled to see them perform it live in this small venue. Lead singer Earl Carroll was a gregarious character who firmly believed in audience participation. Dancing through the crowd while singing, leaving behind the rest of his group, Earl pulled me out on to the floor with him. As our own group's dance captain, I gave him more than he bargained for when I did the splits in the middle of the cheering crowd. It was a night to remember and I'm still reminded of it by my friend Tony Moretti who was there all those years ago, laughing like a drain at the spectacle of me risking ripping my pants in front of one of our favourite acts.

While the Cooper gigs and the booming local music scene in the New York suburbs were tremendous fun, Mount Vernon's Mellotones wanted, and firmly believed we deserved, much more. Levister had worked with us to create something special and we were ready to take it to the next level. And it was about to happen.

Jimmy Jones (top) and the Pretenders

Chapter 3

You Can Call Me Al

A 16 year old singer in 1956 might dream of having an appointment at a record label on Broadway, right next to the Ed Sullivan Theatre. It's exactly where your teenage imagination would locate it. And it's exactly what happened. Pretty much, anyway.

Herald Records wasn't a big label, but boy did it know about our kind of music. The company had been started in Elizabeth, NJ in 1950 by Fred Mendelsohn, a former talent scout and songwriter for Savoy Records. Mendelsohn was a blues fan at heart, but that changed within a couple of years when he needed more capital and teamed up with two guys who had been pressing records for him from a basement in Greenwich Village. Al Silver and his brother-in-law, Jack Angel, encouraged the founder to branch out into vocal groups, while keeping Herald's blues heritage alive by signing Texas legend Lightnin' Hopkins.

Although not a musician himself, Abraham S. Silver had lived and breathed music from an early age. Growing up in Providence RI, he had lived very close to a historically African American Baptist church and become enthralled by its glorious singing. It was therefore no surprise that after Mendelsohn moved on, Al signed

Faye Adams, a gospel singer from Newark NJ, who shot straight to number 1 in the US R&B charts with the Joe Morris-penned *Shake A Hand.* Emboldened by this early success, he trusted his ear for vocal harmonies and signed, in very short order, acts such as the Turbans, the Nutmegs and, of course, the Five Satins across both Herald and its sister label, Ember. These artists became staples of the R&B scene and by the time we met Al in early 1957, so was Herald. Before we even turned up at his office we could picture the name "Mellotones" at the bottom of a Herald record, its yellow label topped with a black trumpet with a banner hanging from it, positioned above the center hole.

The Herald opportunity had arisen from singing in an amateur show in Yonkers, where we were doing covers of current hits. A guy in the audience liked what he saw, approached Dick at the end and said he was going to call up the record company to tell them to see us. Within two weeks we had a meeting. It's been suggested that the audience member was a songwriter named Joe, whose last name has long since been forgotten, and that he promised to arrange an audition for us if we would reciprocate by using it to sing one of his songs. On that basis he would introduce us to Al Silver. 'Joe' may well have been a songwriter – we never got to know – but there was no question of singing anything by him for Herald.

******

On what turned out to be possibly the most important day of our career, the five of us met at the Lincoln Lounge on Mount Vernon's W Lincoln Avenue. The classic Italian trattoria was a favourite haunt of ours and owned by Mr and Mrs Solano, whose son Bobby was at school with me all the way through. Levister eventually swung by, as if we were just meeting for a regular rehearsal – he

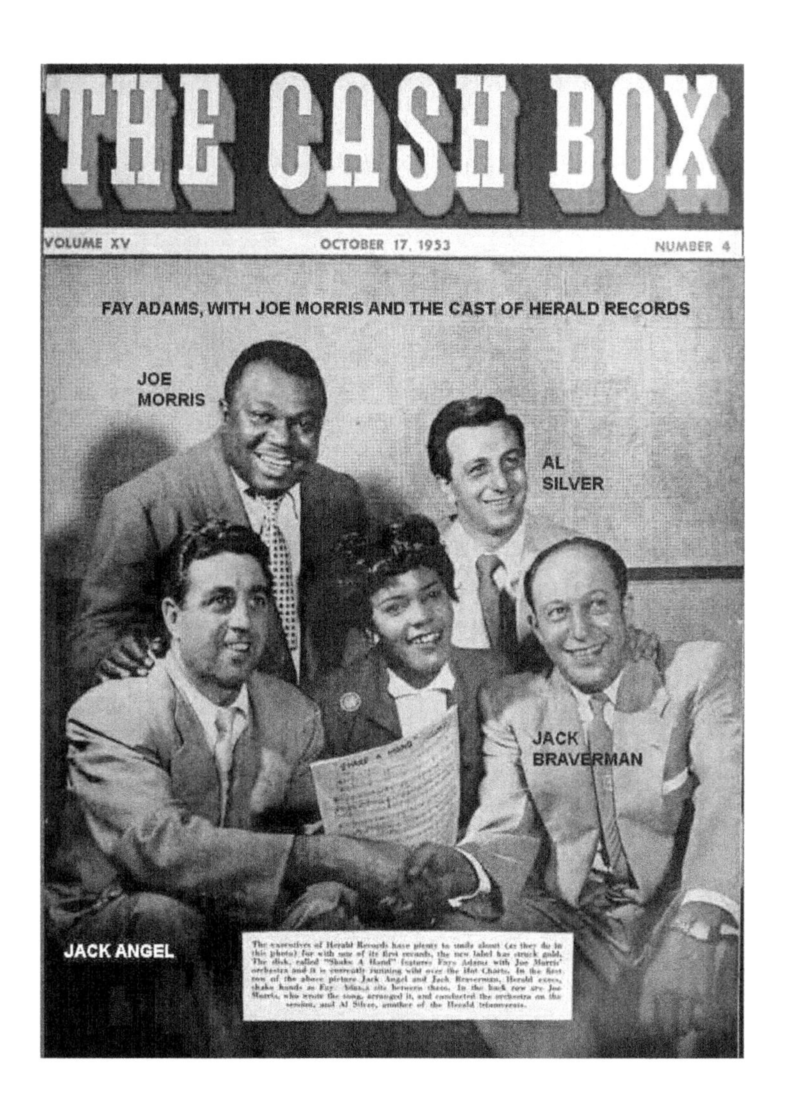

Cash Box had reversed the labels on Silver and Angel

never got particularly excited – and together we made our way to Manhattan.

1697 Broadway was a doorway on the left hand side of the same building as the Ed Sullivan Theater, from which The Late Show with Stephen Colbert is now broadcast. We entered the brown, almost Gothic-looking arched entrance and followed the corridor to Herald's small reception area. This was where songwriters would hang out, waiting to run their work past the label guys and, hopefully, sell them the publishing rights. We shuffled in, casually dressed and, I would guess, looking like a distinctly unimpressive and diverse bunch of kids accompanied by a well turned-out, more mature black man. After buzzing through to the office, the receptionist said simply: "Mr Silver will see you now."

Sitting behind the paper-strewn desk of a businessman and record man in equal measure was a suave but smiley dark haired man in his early forties. He was reasonably welcoming but, as he reminded us more than once in the months that followed, time was money, so we got straight down to it.

"Hey guys, what have you got for me?" said Al, quickly surveying us one by one while maintaining his smile.

All our auditions were *a capella* and there was certainly no role for Dick as we stood awkwardly in that small office. We looked at each other very briefly, nodded and broke into Frankie Lymon's smash hit "Why Do Fools Fall in Love?". Although also only 14 years old, Jerry didn't share Frankie's soprano range; nonetheless, his high tenor, backed by our flawless harmonies, more than did the song justice. The connoisseur of black R&B was visibly impressed. He stood up, revealing his relatively modest height, and moved around a little as he began to think.

Al Silver at the record press

"Give me another one, maybe something a little slower."

More quick nodding between us and we moved right on to The Platters' *Only You*. We were five teenagers who loved the thrill of performing on a stage and getting attention from girls - it was the rock and roll dream; but the technical perfection and accuracy of modern harmony was what really turned us on. Two minutes later, Al was back behind the desk, assessing us once more, running his eyes over the group from left to right.

"I love you guys," he said, "I want to sign you up."

And it was as simple as that. That's how the Mellotones got a record deal.

******

Later that day, celebrating back at the Lincoln Lounge, the boys were jubilant. I, however, couldn't help feeling a little short-changed. If it was that easy to get signed, then why hadn't we set our sights a little higher than Herald? Not that there was anything wrong with the set up there: Al had said everything we could have hoped for and they seemed like a professional outfit; they had also issued some huge hits in a short space of time, punching way above their weight. Others we would meet and work with at Herald would soon make us feel out of our depth. Perhaps the confidence I had, both in my own voice and in the quality of what we and Dick had put together, had made me slightly arrogant.

"Why don't we go to Capitol, or Decca?" I suddenly lobbed into the triumphant conversation, like a grenade with the pin still fixed. Levister was also avoiding unnecessary exuberance, but that was just his way. My unwelcome sanity-check of the situation was largely ignored; the boys just wanted to get started and I figured there was no pursuing this line of argument any further. We were on our way and the contracts were in the mail.

When the paperwork arrived, I was the last to get it signed by his parents – remember, we were still minors. I had no further hesitations, but my dad added his usual friction to the process. In the end he had no choice. Realistically he wasn't going to stop a record deal in its tracks, not least because he couldn't come up with a good reason why I shouldn't be a successful pop singer.

"Neil, you've finally got your wish!" my mom said, genuinely delighted for me. I, too, was delighted, having moved on from my misgivings about not sharing a label with Dean Martin and Frank Sinatra. I was now a recording artist.

Fully contracted to Herald, with a deal giving each of us 5 cents per record, it was no more than three weeks before we were back in Broadway to meet the man who gave us one of the best-loved doo-wop songs of all time. William Myles Nobles – professionally known as Billy Myles, was a staff songwriter for Herald, one of the main guys you would find in the lobby with something new for Al. He had three or four songs ready for us to try out, an arrangement that felt flattering and, in a way, promoted us to 'grown-up recording star' status. At the same time we were naturally apprehensive about what this experienced tunesmith in his early thirties was going to put in front of us. The short menu of possibilities didn't excite us at first, but then the choice of song wasn't only ours. In the same year, Billy penned a great song that we loved, but Al thought it wasn't right for us. "The Joker (That's What They Call Me)" was recorded by Billy himself a few months after, giving the writer a huge hit in both the R&B and pop charts.

There was something about *Tonite, Tonite* that grabbed us immediately. At our core we were a ballad group; kids, but with a musical taste beyond our years. Although as a five-piece (not individually) we had been influenced by Frankie Lymon and the Teenagers – and their success had definitely sparked interest in us as an unusual 'white R&B version' – there was nothing remotely 'kid-sound' about *Tonite, Tonite*. Once we had become part of the scene around Herald, with Jerry still singing lead we started getting told that the Mellotones sounded a little *too* like the Teenagers. That was a major reason for Bobby beginning to front the group.

We took the song home and for the next two weeks subjected it to the Levister treatment of painstaking rehearsal, note by note, trying different harmonies until Dick was satisfied it couldn't sound any better. We virtually lived in that practice room at the Mount

Vernon Boys' Club in every hour we weren't at school, or in my case, playing basketball. The upstairs room in the club's original premises on 10th Avenue had a piano for Dick and he arranged to meet us there at 7pm every night for two hours, but we spent way more than that time every week rehearsing.

Dick eventually called Al.

"I think we're ready to bring it to you and show you what we've done with it," said our manager as he called Al at his home, phoning from the boys' club. Working in rock and roll in the middle of its first explosion wasn't a nine-to-five thing; I guess it still isn't.

"OK, I'll have Leroy look at it," replied Al. "Get the boys to come in again."

Leroy Kirkland, an extremely experienced musician of about 50, was a superb arranger who would prove to be critical to shaping our sound. Looking back, we were extremely privileged to have him involved with the group. A cool, confident and well-dressed guy, Leroy was no ordinary session guitarist. We were in the right place at the right time because he had also been playing with the Five Satins on Herald's sister label, Ember. Beyond doo-wop, however, he had worked with both Tommy and Jimmy Dorsey in the 1940s and recorded with Etta James, Charlie Parker and Ella Fitzgerald, as well as playing in Alan Freed's Rock and Roll Shows. After helping us out in the studio, Leroy went on to become one of the mid-20th century's most sought-after composers of Black R&B music after Otis Blackwell and Jesse Stone. Music fans have commented over the years on the great guitarist they heard on our records. That was Leroy.

Back at Herald we were taken down the hall to a rehearsal room of quite a decent size. We had previously seen the Moonglows - who were not Herald artists but signed to Chess through Alan Freed – rehearsing their dance moves in that room, as taught by R&B choreographer Cholly Atkins. Situated behind a large, black music stand was Leroy. As we ran through the number, over and over again, he would make weird movements and facial expressions to say 'step it up', or 'bring it down a little'. He was clearly a perfectionist and, while we were used to being drilled by Levister to produce excellence, we were now in the big league.

Soon the song was off Leroy's desk and back on to the boss's – and he loved it. "We have to cut this straight away," said Al, almost literally rubbing his hands at the thought of getting us into the studio. We were a little bit different and he was impatient for our recording debut so that he could effectively launch our career under his wing. When Al said straight away, he was serious. He made a few calls and we were booked in for our first real studio visit. When we left the Herald office, out in the lobby was a young songwriter who turned out to be the great Bob Crewe.

"I heard what you guys were doing in there," he said. "I really like your sound – I'm going to write you some songs." It wouldn't be too long before we heard from him again.

******

The moment had arrived! We were in the studio to lay down our first tracks. But not just in any studio: Al had booked us into Bell Sound, New York's busiest independent studio and the recording venue of choice for hitmakers of that time. Located on 46th and 8th, Bell Sound had been established in 1950 by radio mechanics Al Weintraub and Dan Cronin. It was at Bell's previous premises on West 89th Street that the million seller *Shake A Hand* had been recorded. Al Silver's artists grew to become regulars at Bell. Especially meaningful for us was that in December 1955 Frankie Lymon had recorded *Why Do Fools* there, accompanied by Jimmy Wright's bluesy tenor sax. The big record labels I admired also used Bell to complement their own studios. In 1957, the year we were there, Decca boss Bob Thiele brought in the McGuire Sisters to record *Sugar Time* with a 16-piece band. Dion and the Belmonts made *Tell Me Why* and the Monotones cut the doo-wop classic *The Book of Love* with the unmistakeable single hit on the bass drum behind the microphones. Legend has it that during the recording, a baseball ball flew into the studio and made a thud. The noise was noticed during the sound control, but it seemed to fit as a bass drum replacement and was left on the track. In the years that followed, Buddy Holly, The Drifters, Lloyd Price, Del Shannon and just about anybody you can think of from that time made their music at Bell Sound. The place had a reputation for being able to capture atmosphere and excitement on vinyl.

The premises were surprisingly large, possibly because in the mid-Fifties they had to accommodate more 'real' musicians, as opposed to artificial instruments created by a synthesiser or even a mixing desk. If a track involved string and horn sections alongside the usual drums, bass, guitar and keyboards, plus singers, the place could get pretty crowded. Recording sessions lasted, on average, three hours, which would normally be long enough to get four songs in the can before the next group came in. In fact, the slots were closely monitored by the Musicians Union to make sure that overtime was paid. Time was money, and not just for Al Silver. In addition to Leroy, Bell Sound§ hosted a regular gang of session musicians who could be relied upon for the minimum number of run-throughs. These included Mickey Baker on guitar, Panama Francis on drums and the much-requested Sam 'The Man' Taylor on sax. If strings were needed, orchestral arranger Sammy Lowe was called in.

The first session in April 1957 saw us record four songs:

Tonite, Tonite – released as Herald 502
Do Baby Do – the flip side, composed by Levister
Baby Tell Me Why, Why, Why – released as Herald 511, by Levister with two Herald staffers
The Only Girl (I'll Ever Love) – the flip side, written by Levister and Eddie

It was a relief that our efforts recording *Tonite, Tonite* would later produce a good return: 'no pain, no gain' doesn't begin to describe that part of the studio session. To be fair, we were all new at this game, but it was torture for Bobby at first. As lead singer, he was located in his own glass booth away from the rest of us. We couldn't see him at all. There were various technical and engineer types running around, but one unnamed guy – in hindsight, I guess the producer – was ultimately responsible for delivering the finished product. He was losing patience with Bobby, who in turn was getting very frustrated, even annoyed at the relentless prodding and gesturing at him to put more feeling into his vocal performance. I guess we were now working at a different level of professionalism required for recording, despite our hard work in preparation. We (and Al) had expected to wrap up *Tonite, Tonite* in no more than three takes. Failing to please the grumpy producer meant that it took us nine attempts.

"I'm paying for this! Don't screw it up!" protested Al before we were finally done with the first song. My own disappointment was that the full impact of the wonderful harmonies was toned down on the final recording to give slightly more prominence to Bobby's vocal. In my opinion that was a mistake.

The second recording session was within a short few weeks, in May 1957, and completed the output of the Mello-Kings in their original line-up. The songs from both sessions weren't necessarily released in line with the order in which they were laid down in the studio. This time we recorded:

Sassafrass – written by Bob Crewe and Frank Slay, and issued as H-507
Chapel on the Hill – another Billy Myles composition, for the flip side

Our Love is Beautiful – written by Eddie and Dick, and issued in 1960 as H-548
Love at First Sight – by J.Tarter, not issued until 1961 as H-567

Later to become famous for producing and co-writing with Bob Gaudio a string of Top Ten hits for Frankie Valli and the Four Seasons, Bob Crewe was already well established in a songwriting partnership with young Texan pianist Frank Slay when we had bumped into him at Herald. A lean, good looking guy of 27, with a shock of blond hair and enormous confidence, Bob was very clearly destined for huge success in the music business. Despite his lack of formal musical training, he had a great ear for what would work and was a good enough singer to test and perform his own creations before handing them on to various groups. He originally wrote the smash *Silhouettes* for us, which would have made an incredible follow up to *Tonite, Tonite*. On calling Al Silver to tell him about it, Bob learned that we were touring around Baltimore and DC for the next two weeks. He couldn't wait, so instead gave it to The Rays, a group he had heard auditioning at around the same time. They took it to number three on both the R&B and Pop charts in 1957.

So we got *Sassafrass*. A jaunty, upbeat number in which we 'spelled' the crazy title when singing the chorus. It pains me to admit that a song written for us by Bob Crewe is still one of my least favourite Mello-Kings tracks. Nonetheless it had some great guitar work from Leroy – nice palm muting in the intro and slick soloing – and the end result was well packaged. And so it should have been, given the time we spent on it. Rather like *Tonite, Tonite*, we took forever to get the song right; this time not because we were perfecting lush harmonies, but as a result of our inconsistent spelling between takes.

Bob Crewe (top left) and Frank Slay with The Rays, 1957

By contrast, Chapel on the Hill, on the other side of the record, was perhaps my favourite. Unsurprising, given my love of ballads and the singing heroes I'd grown up with. I'd even go as far as saying I still prefer it to *Tonite, Tonite*. Either way, I guess Billy Myles was more my kind of writer. *Chapel* was another romantic, slow-dance number, with soft jazzy guitar sweeps, swooning horns and – the best bit for me – a short oboe solo. I loved that part; I think it might have been the first time I'd ever heard an oboe and it was on our record making a beautiful, slightly sad little statement in the middle.

Tonite, Tonite b/w Do Baby Do was pressed with us named on the label as the Mellotones. It was only after about three thousand copies were sitting in their sleeves that Al Silver realized there was another doo-wop group of the same name. Someone, perhaps even the five of us, should have known about Jerry Carr and the Mello-Tones, who were to release their song *Rosie Lee* on the Gee label in the same month. Eddie Quinn and I quickly came up with the Mello-Kings. Another myth about us is that the "King" part came from Dick Levister's middle name, with which he had also named his King Levister orchestra. That wasn't the case.

Eddie and I loved to goof about and one thing guaranteed to set us off during rehearsals was Levister's rather eccentric way of expressing his dissatisfaction. After putting his hands over his face, he would shake his head repeatedly and shout "Stop it, stop it, stop it!" in his inimitable gravelly voice. This would happen several times during practice as we were made to harmonise over a single note over and over again. After a while, Eddie and I decided that Levister's unintentionally comedic performance reminded us of Kingfish, the Tim Moore character in TV's *Amos and Andy*. Our nickname for him became shortened to 'King' and then helped to provide a last-minute renaming for the group.

In any event, even after two pressings, some copies still bore the Mellotones name. Needless to say, these are now rarities with considerable value.

Success with the first record was a slow burn for a number of reasons, mostly to do with confusion over our name and which song was being marketed. The April 1957 first pressing called us the Mellotones; the next pressing had Mellotones on one side and Mello-Kings on the other. Then there was a lack of clarity on which was the A side. The two songs were very different styles. A review of the promo copy on 18 May 1957 in Cash Box, the music industry trade magazine, perceived *Do Baby Do* as the release, calling it "a novelty r & r with a western tang … that could push the group right into the big money. A quick beat jumper with a strong, individual sound and a wax that bears close watching. It has all the elements that the teeners require. Stay close to this exuberant bouncer." Levister was very pleased with this review of his composition, in his usual controlled way.

It was a different story with *Tonite, Tonite*. In the same review, Cash Box labelled it "a slow beat ballad blues, well done. The Mello-Kings turn out an excellent wax – but one that is too much in the vein of too many things already offered [to] the public. Could get plenty of attention, but in the final analysis it will be *Do Baby Do*."

How wrong could Cash Box have been? While it only ever peaked at #77 on the Billboard Hot 100, *Tonite, Tonite* stayed on the chart for 11 weeks between August and November 1957 and sold more than three million copies.

In the early days of the song charting, Bill Myles said to us during another visit to Herald: "Do you guys even know anything about Billboard magazine? I gave you a hit record!"

Tonite, Tonite

The pressing in widest circulation – much rarer with 'Mellotones'

In some ways even better than briefly hitting #1, *Tonite, Tonite* has been voted one of the top three doo-wop songs of all time, alongside the Five Satins' *In the Still of the Night*, and The Penguins' *Earth Angel*. Covered by Dion and the Belmonts, as well as by Frankie Valli and the Four Seasons, our hit is still considered one of the most popular group harmony recordings of the era.

Chapter 4

We Have Lift Off!

PLAYING the famous Apollo Theater in Harlem, Manhattan, was possibly the pinnacle of my musical career, for many reasons. Sure, the Mello-Kings played some amazing auditoriums and prestigious broadcast sessions, but the Apollo had to be the most cool.

Built in 1913, the Apollo on W 125th Street started life as a music hall with a Whites Only entry policy. It's ironic that from the swing era to this day, it has been associated with African American performers. It's presently the home of Showtime at the Apollo, a nationally syndicated TV variety showcasing new talent. We were well-known by the time we appeared there for our first show on October 4, 1957, but what made us most proud was being one of the first white pop acts to walk on to its stage. In a way we felt validated as a genuine doo-wop act in an almost exclusively black musical genre.

There is quite a debate around the Apollo's first white pop act. In the 1940s, white acts such as bandleaders Harry James, Woody Herman and Charlie Barnet had appeared there with great success. They were followed by modern jazz greats such as Dave Brubeck, Stan Getz and Buddy Rich. Weekend shows played to a predominantly white audience. But doo-wop and rock and roll had grown directly from black music, so when we played in Harlem at arguably the peak of this musical revolution, it would have been natural for the theatre to reach first for artists from that community. Urban myth has it that Buddy Holly was the first white rock and roll act to play the Apollo, a few weeks before us on August 16, 1957. However, Dale Hawkins played there in July 1957, while Jimmy Cavallo and the House Rockers appear to have been first in December 1956.

Jerry Lee Lewis beat us by only a week. Anyway, it was still very unusual. Alongside us on the bill were fellow doo-woppers the original Del Vikings, R&B alto sax supremo Earl Bostic, comedic multi-instrumentalist and inventor of his own "Vout-o-Reenee" singing language, Slim Gaillard, plus the Tunedrops, Varetta Dillard and Reuben Phillips. There was something else important that we had in common with Buddy Holly: we believed we had been booked assuming we were black; Apollo audiences at the start of Buddy's six-night run had thought they were seeing an R&B group called the Crickets.

Irv Nahan had secured us the booking, clearly not having given the Apollo the full picture about us. Certainly not a picture they could look at, in any case. Irv had been extremely effective in getting us work; he was very energetic and extraordinarily well connected in the music business. I remember very well the day Al Silver introduced us to him at Herald's offices. Al had set up a meeting because, as a white vocal-harmony group, we were still a rarity and if anyone could help to get us exposure alongside other major acts, it was Irv.

By that time he had already contributed substantially to the success of The Drifters, working with George Treadwell and Lewis Lebish to manage the group. Soon after he became a one-third shareholder in The Drifters Inc.

Those were the days when touring supported record sales; now, in the age of streaming music and digital downloads, it's the complete opposite. Most of the money for groups who don't write their own songs seems to be made from months on the road playing huge stadiums all over the world. Irv was well organised and had a proven methodology for getting groups into theaters. He dealt almost exclusively with black R&B acts but, working with legendary promoter Irving Feld, he would put mainly Top Ten artists together on one 'package' bill and tour it for 30 days. In this way he launched Jackie Wilson as solo artist, straight after he left The Dominoes. He also included Paul Anka as a regular fixture, which was how we got to play on the same nights as the great singer, who is still performing today.

A business-like, robust looking guy in his forties, dark haired and well-dressed, Irv was very polite and straightforward. He didn't need to meet us for long before he was convinced that we would fit well in his package and would offer something different. Five white boys who only sang and already had a following. Why not?

"I can do something with you guys," Irv said very simply. "I think you're great and I can get you a lot of work. Let's do it." He smiled in a friendly way, nodded to himself a few times in the same way the talent scouts had done in my kitchen years before, presumably to say that Al had been right to bring him in, then got up and left. He very soon turned out to be true to his word.

We were booked for six nights at the Apollo, beginning on a Friday. It was an early evening show but, as anyone who's been in the music business will tell you, there was a lot of hanging around and we had to be there by 1pm. Since it was a schoolday, it involved me skipping (yet again) Mr Caville's business class. Dressed casually in jeans and a shirt, I left school for the train to Grand Central Station, after which I would walk the several blocks to Harlem. The streets around the theater had a reputation for being rough. That may have been based on a mistrust of the local black community, but I never felt uncomfortable. I had a good number of black friends in Mount Vernon, many of whom played basketball with me. It was no big deal. For no particular reason, The Mello-Kings (possibly with the exception of brothers Bobby and Jerry) usually travelled separately to their shows. Later we shared our own car, but for the Apollo we turned up individually.

Strictly speaking, we had played at the Apollo before, in one of their occasional 'Amateur Hour' shows. These were brutal little gigs, with an unforgiving audience and a tough audition to be selected. Taking part in these basement try-outs was a white kid who, these days, we might describe as having learning difficulties. Challenged was the word we used then. His singing was terrible and we wondered why he was there, vying with a bunch of better qualified performers to enter the lion's den. To everyone's surprise, he was allowed through. It gets worse. The MC for these shows was a bizarrely attired character with a large golden hook protruding from his sleeve – but this weird looking black guy with cruel, laughing eyes was not dressed as a comedy pirate. Those who passed the audition were called on to the stage and gave it their best shot in front of an unkind crowd. If they - or even just the MC - didn't like what they saw, the hook was deployed to drag the budding artist back into the wings, to the great amusement of the house. We watched from the side as that poor kid, probably not fully aware of what was going on, was pilloried by the crowd before being pulled off, unceremoniously.

That awful experience in the same theatre did little to dampen our excitement months later. Nor did our dressing room, which was no more than a shitty, smelly place at the top of the theater, an area that was busy with artists and their teams running around with costumes, make up and other paraphernalia. There was no complimentary food and drink for performers. Stars of today, with complex dietary requirements, whimsical demands and contractual riders would have felt very unloved. The others on the bill didn't make any effort to engage with us at all. Earl Bostic, an influential old school jazzer, by then in his mid-forties and trying to widen his appeal, shot us looks that made us feel as if a bunch of white teenagers didn't belong on stage at the Apollo. Perhaps we were just self-conscious. Slim Gaillard was no more friendly, despite his comical demeanor. Unaccompanied by Irv or Dick, we were very much on our own. In fact we didn't see Irv more than twice after our meeting at Herald.

Another factor that made us feel different from the two all-black vocal groups was our outfits. Malcolm Dodds and the Tunedrops wore colourful plaid coats and black bow ties, while the Del-Vikings sported baby-pink tuxedos. We thought we were looking very sharp in white jackets, with black shirts, white ties, black pants and white bucks, but somehow it seemed a little conservative and unexciting compared with our fellow acts. To be fair, sometimes we wore red jackets with black satin lapels, but not at the Apollo. Dick had originally come up with the idea of white jackets – it was

a look he favored while performing in his regular work – but it was Larry who adapted it. While a student at Edison, Larry had a part-time job with a tailor in Mount Vernon who taught him the basics of sewing and cutting. Larry designed and shaped the 'M' logo and black diamond that was positioned under the left breast pocket of our jackets. It was a neat addition that turned an outfit into effectively a uniform and we were proud to wear it.

her first Groove Record
A TWO-SIDED SMASH
Varetta Dillard
DARLING, LISTEN TO THE WORDS OF THIS SONG
MAMA DON'T WANT
(WHAT PAPA DON'T WANT)
GROOVE 0139; 4G-0139
GROOVE RECORDS
155 EAST 24th STREET NEW YORK

I'm often asked if the Mello-Kings had a routine before going on stage: a vocal warm-up, perhaps singing scales; a pep talk from Bobby, since he was the 'lead' singer; a collective whooping accompanied by some dance moves. No, there was never anything of the sort. Very occasionally, we'd sing a few bars of a number we were about to perform, but we were always good to go. Our rehearsals with Dick between shows kept us exceptionally well prepared at all times. Despite this precocious professionalism and confidence, we were always very jovial and a little giggly at showtime. On that Friday night, however, we were nervous as hell before walking on to the Apollo's stage for the first time. It wasn't made any easier by opening the show, since we were the most 'junior' act in every sense of the word. Would Captain Hook suddenly appear if we bombed?

Watching from the wings, we saw house lights dim and a spotlight appear near the middle of the stage.

"This is it!" chirped Eddie. "Let's not screw it up!"

There was no great pizzazz before the first act at the Apollo; the MC just got straight down to it, saying: "Please welcome, from Mount Vernon, the Mello-Kings." I walked on first from stage right, as I usually did, to stand on the left of the group as the audience viewed us. The murmuring, whispering audience was a little confused that night. "What's with the white teens?" I guess they were saying as they nudged each other, possibly disappointed not to be treated to the next Frankie Lymon. We felt there was a hill to climb in winning them over, but to be honest, we knew we were good and they'd soon come around.

Straight into *Do Baby Do.* The same house band accompanied all the acts. Of course, they were at least as good as anyone who ever played on our records – hey, this was the Apollo! The song is relatively uptempo, with a swingy, bluesy guitar solo; dancers could do a slow-to-steady jive to *Do Baby Do.* The solo section allowed us to indulge in a little choreography. I say 'us', but I mean me and Eddie, since Bobby, Jerry and Larry, while they were great singers, were no movers. I put together basic steps and arm gestures for those guys to go with most of the songs we performed, but Eddie and I took care of the more energetic stuff. In this case, Eddie would lift me into the air and I would come down to finish in a splits position. He'd then push my head as I repeatedly rose and lowered myself to the floor. This never failed to delight audiences and the Apollo's on that first night was no exception. Just that effort to add a physical aspect that might not have been expected of a white vocal group was very well received.

Next, *Tonite, Tonite.* This was a song they knew instantly after its extensive airplay, yet didn't necessarily associate with us. No dance antics with our love song, but the harmonies were flawless and the crowd went as wild as we might have hoped when we finished. It can't have been often that the opening act at the Apollo got two curtain calls. The theater recognized that and we moved further up the bill for the remaining five nights.

Adrenalin pumping, we felt triumphant coming off that stage and each of us must have had beaming grins etched on our faces for a full 24 hours until we returned to the same Harlem spotlight. The Apollo had fulfilled our wildest dreams and there was no sense of anti-climax whatsoever. We felt ready and able to perform anywhere after that and nothing would faze us. The Mello-Kings had been up there with the best and we'd been a hit with one of the most uncompromising audiences in America.

The only dent in our offstage high was what became an all too familiar after-show conversation with the AGVA guys. The American Guild of Variety Actors is still an entertainment union representing performers in variety entertainment, from Las Vegas cabaret to circuses, theme parks and comedy shows. AGVA was the successor to the American Federation of Actors organized by actress and singer Sophie Tucker and others in the late 1930s. Normally working in pairs, one with some kind of ledger book, the AGVA guys collected performers' 'dues' onsite, after acts had been paid and before a theater closed for the night. Needless to say, as five teenagers we were reluctant to pay a healthy slice of our new earnings for this protection, not least because we didn't remember signing up for AGVA in the first place. Anyway, there didn't seem to be any choice and it was just the way things were done.

Earl Bostic, 1957

Even so, we were paid $850, in cash, between five of us for the six nights. That's more than $8,500 in 2022 money and compared well with the still not badly paid dates we did on Irv's package tours around the eastern half of the US. He took 10 per cent.

******

Back in Mount Vernon, I briefly resumed my 'normal' life as a basketball playing teenager, albeit with more dough in my pocket. I celebrated our latest success by treating all my buddies to pizza at Scuderi's on Gramatan Avenue. Oh, the rock 'n' roll lifestyle! Best of all, though, I'm still in touch with some of the guys from round that table. The check for that evening was nothing compared to the gift I bought myself. Every day in 'Apollo week' I passed a fancy shoe store close to the theater. My friends had always worn better shoes than me: my parents could only afford to buy me shoes from Thom McAn; I was lucky even to get some real Converse sneakers for basketball. After six days, a good chunk of my new riches from harmonising were blown on the most beautiful shoes that, at 17 years old, I had ever seen. Black loafers with a dark gray suede panel in the middle. I parted with $50, which was half the average guy's weekly earnings in 1957, and carried the shoes home, guarding them with my life.

Chapter 5

The Guy with the Goods

IF I were forced to pick a favourite tour I spent with the Mello-Kings, it would have to be the week we spent playing the Uptown Theater in Philadelphia in summer 1957. It may not have been as iconic as the Apollo, or as different from home as our later trip to Chicago, but it sure as hell was the most fun.

While the opportunity had been created by Irv Nahan, we wouldn't have appeared without the blessing of one of America's most influential DJs at the time, George Woods. Aged around 30, Woods was only slightly older than Dick Clark and their paths had crossed many times in the early years of their careers. Both had started out in New York, but Woods was originally born in Georgia before moving to Harlem as a child. He became one of the first African Americans on a mainstream media outlet when he joined New York City station WWRL in 1952, heading for WHAT in Philadelphia after only a few months then to rival WDAS in 1956. Woods's twin motivations of breaking new R&B acts and championing the civil rights movement converged in the year the Mello-Kings met him when his support helped propel singer and activist Sam Cooke's *You Send Me* to the top of the charts.

Energetic and popular beyond the black community, Woods became nicknamed 'The Guy with the Goods' for his ability always to deliver, whether it was a great radio show, help for an artist or rounding up several top acts for a concert. Dick Clark, his *Bandstand* neighbor in Philly, is said to have relied heavily on Woods to advise him on which records were popular with black audiences when he tried to broaden the appeal of his conspicuously 'white' show.

Effectively as a much a promoter as a broadcaster, it was no surprise that Woods had become well acquainted with Irv, who was by then a major conduit for booking R&B acts. Like other relationships with agents, this one was a win-win. Woods was able to attract some of the biggest names in rock 'n' roll and could fill several major venues every night, many times over. The Mello-Kings were booked for a week at North Philadelphia's Uptown Theater, part of an informal network of black theaters that hosted concerts in the East and Midwest, including New York's Apollo Theater, Washington D.C.'s Howard Theater, Baltimore's Royal Theater, Detroit's Fox Theater, and Chicago's Regal. We played all of these except Detroit. Together they became known as the 'Chitlin' Circuit', after chitterlings, the soul food dish, as they became synonymous with providing commercial and cultural outlets for African American musicians, comedians, and other entertainers during the segregation era. Woods called the Uptown "the grand jewel of entertainment for Black America", while R&B singer Ruth Brown said that you had to play there to prove that you had made it as an entertainer.

But first you had to be 'quality controlled' by Woods. We had been told to go to see him the day before the gig, complete with our outfits. Not so much an audition, but a sense-check that he hadn't booked a terrible act. He did this with everyone scheduled to perform, but in this case he showed a particular interest in us because he had heard we were white. It was a similar situation to our Apollo experience: the promoter had to see it to believe it. We showed up at the theatre with all our stuff (but without Levister) and were directed to a single, large dressing room with lockers. A 16 year old Paul Anka was already in there, fresh from having released his smash hit 'Diana'. He pretty much ignored us. We did the same. Small talk and pleasantries weren't really for teenagers and, although he was already a bigger star than us, we weren't particularly impressed to meet him. While he would soon have a huge, all-age audience, he looked like a kid and there were five of us, slightly older and altogether looking more cool.

Walking out on to the stage, we were met by the unusual sight of George Woods sitting in a large, almost throne-like chair, on a platform that looked down on us. He was a handsome, suave looking guy, well dressed but relaxed in a sport coat and open neck shirt. All the time we were on the stage, Woods didn't say a single word. When we looked ready to start, he just nodded, then sat watching impassively, regally, with his hands pressed together in a prayer under his bottom lip. The bizarre pose was frozen, as if the tips of his fingers had been glued to his lower face. Our *a capella* performance of *Tonite, Tonite* forced just the slightest hint of a sign that he was impressed. We could see it in his eyes as he seemed to suppress a positive reaction, damned if he was going to show he liked our act. He was probably itching to tap his foot as we sang *Do Baby Do*, but his shoes remained fixed to the platform below. After the briefest of pauses when the song ended, Woods nodded again and we took that as a signal of both approval and time to exit. Then he finally opened his mouth to say: "I'll see you tomorrow." We hadn't been at all intimidated by the less-than-friendly audition process. The Mello-Kings had enormous confidence in their performance at all times. Our harmonies were always fine-tuned and, frankly, near as dammit perfect. In these close-up situations, with only a promoter or arranger listening, we would blow our audience away and were invariably told that we were 'better than the record'.

******

Levister had kindly arranged for the five us to stay with a lady relative of his in Philly. She had a reasonably large house in a nice neighborhood and hosted us very generously, feeding us well and driving us to the theatre throughout the week. This saved us a lot of money, since hotels, transport and any other costs of touring were usually taken off our earnings by the record company. I shared a room with Eddie, as was often the case. One night we had an unexpected visitor, a girl of no more than 17 who had discovered where the Mello-Kings were staying. We originally thought she had been to the show at the Uptown and afterwards trailed us back to the house, but later reckoned she knew the family and had been tipped off.

Eddie and I were asleep. When we finished shows, the group generally returned to the hotel or wherever we were staying and, after a few laughs, we'd go to bed at a relatively respectable time. Philly was no exception, especially since we were staying with 'real adults', and in any event we were usually exhausted from a truly punishing schedule. That night my pal and I were fast asleep at around 11pm when the girl swung by, making her way to our room either through an open window or, in hindsight, possibly even having been allowed in through the front door. What happened next was a little surreal and neither of us was fully aware of it until the morning. I don't mean to be ungallant, but our intruder, a white girl, was not at all attractive: plump, dark haired and by no means fair of face. In turn, and what seemed at length, Eddie and I felt the girl's hot and not wholly fragrant breath as she carefully planted kisses on our semi-sleeping faces. Opening one eye, I glimpsed our fan as she sloped off, apparently satisfied with her visit to the Mello-Kings. There was no telling if she'd been looking specifically for Eddie and me or if indeed she'd then gone looking for the others. Thinking Eddie was asleep, and safe in the knowledge that the visitor had gone, I returned to my slumber.

"Did…you…?" ventured Eddie when we woke up the next morning, wondering if this had been a shared experience or something weirdly unique to him.

"Yeah! What was that?"

"Fat slob!"

"Ewwghh!"

We laughed until we almost cried, partly disgusted, partly thrilled by this low-level groupie adventure. It was yucky and hilarious, but still quite 'rock'n'roll'.

******

Our first night went extremely well. Great harmonies, perfect timing and, by way of 'stagecraft', the usual antics from me and Eddie that gave the audience a little extra. As the smallest act in terms of national success at that time, the Mello-Kings had been put on as the opening act. But for one night only: the reaction in the house had impressed Woods and, as the week progressed, we moved from first up to third and then eventually fourth. We had overtaken Paul Anka, who was basking in the glory of a huge national hit. Our record success at the time of playing Philly was confined to the important, but still local charts around the east coast, although our reputation seemed to travel much wider. While we blew kisses to the crowd before leaving the stage, Anka would throw strings of pearls to the girls when he finished his set. These may well have been fake, but it was a lavish gesture that wasn't wasted on his fans.

Our young co-star was less generous, however, when he found out he would be warming up the audience for us. He took to showing up late for performances, hoping his 'unavoidable' tardiness would bump him back up the bill. Bad move. This didn't wash with Woods, a no-nonsense kind of guy who liked to run a tight ship. All acts had to be on time and, once they'd finished their sets, had to stick around backstage ready to reappear eventually for the finale, during which they would each come forward for their curtain call, introduced by the great man himself. Woods took a very dim view of Anka's behavior that week. However, he didn't go as far as our own hothead Eddie, who cornered him in the dressing room later on. Lifting Anka by the collar and off his feet, Eddie threatened to hang him on a hook as he expressed in no uncertain terms his displeasure at the late stunt.

"Hey guys, let's be friends," pleaded Anka. "We can hang out! You can tell me where all these great girls are!"

We had made our point and both acts stayed firmly away from each other after that.

Beyond us and Paul Anka, the first of the other three acts on the bill for 'Philly Week' was a great young soul singer named Donny Elbert. He was about 21 and came from Buffalo, NY, although he'd been born in New Orleans. Donny was an easy going and modest guy who had been the driving force behind a short-lived doo-wop group called the Vibraharps (where did we get these names from in those days?). A talented songwriter, guitarist and arranger, as well as a superb vocalist, he struck out on his own in 1957, the year we played alongside him, and had a national R&B hit with *What Can I Do?* It was a pleasure working with Donny, a true professional who went on to enjoy reasonable success on the soul scene for another 20 years.

Girl group The Bobbettes, by contrast, were younger than us. Kids, really. Two were only 13. Like Paul Anka, who was at first accompanied by his older cousin, they had chaperones on tour with them. Led by sisters Jannie and Emma Pought, the fivesome came

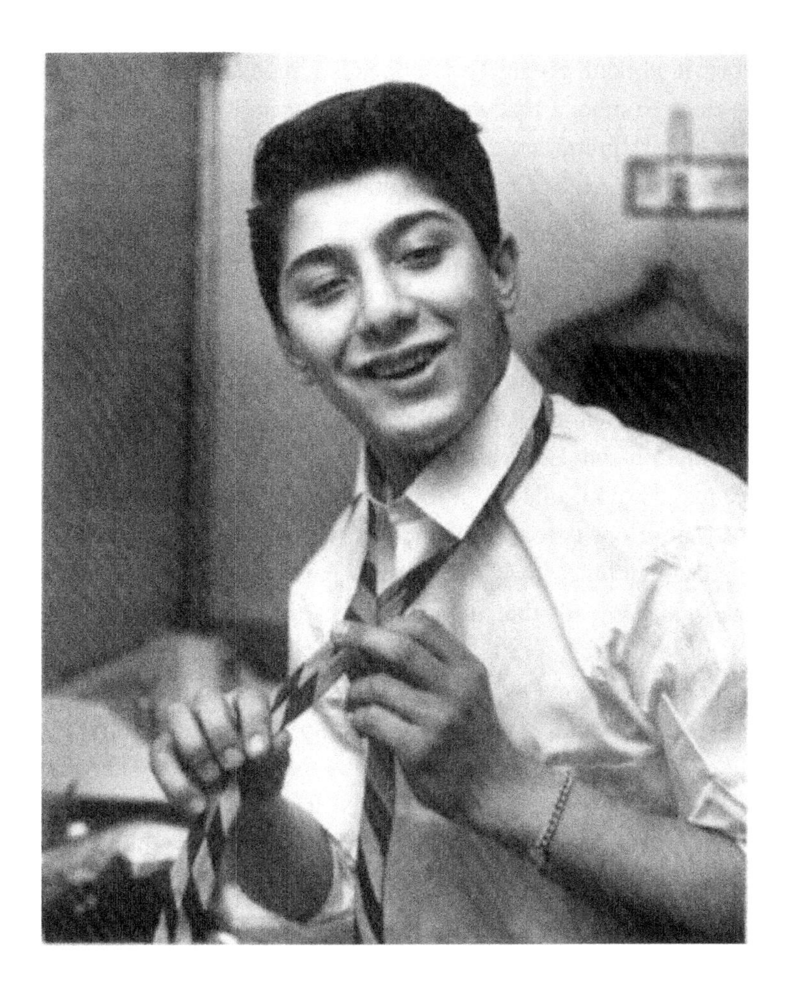

Paul Anka, age 16, on tour in 1957

from East Harlem and had been discovered playing amateur night at The Apollo before getting signed to the famous Atlantic label. Their first single, *Mr. Lee,* was a toned-down cheeky song about their schoolteacher, which was recast by the label as a girl-crush number. It worked, giving The Bobbettes a huge national hit and an R&B chart Number 1 that would later appear high up in lists of the best ever girl group songs. The music wasn't bad, either, with legendary arranger Al Caiola on guitar (kind of their equivalent of Leroy) and star producer Ray Ellis on piano. Cute and looking polished on stage in their yellow polka dot dresses, the girls had classic NY vocal group credentials, having grown up in the projects and practised their skills in hallways and alleys. They were great fun and always goofing around. But nobody on the bill could match the energy, excitement and just sheer craziness of our oldest co-star: Screamin' Jay Hawkins.

We played alongside Jay a few times in '57 and every time he seemed more outrageous than the last. He was a force of nature. Aged 28 at that time, Jay's swagger was based partly on the success he had achieved not that many years earlier as a middleweight boxer, learning his craft in the military, where he had also entertained the troops as a singer. After a short stint in guitarist Teddy Grimes' band, Jay went solo and soon, in 1956, scored his biggest hit with the self-penned *I Put A Spell On You.* The song came to define his stage persona, which was encouraged by Alan Freed as part of his Rock and Roll Revue. Almost overnight, Jay had gone from emotional blues singer to growling, wide-eyed and spooky showman. His favorite stage props included voodoo dolls, which he liked to wear strapped to his wrist, and early versions of strobe lights. While on tour with us he once used these in a scary routine onstage that involved one of his own (numerous) children.

the BOBBETTES
mean BU$INE$$
Current Best Seller
MR. LEE
b/w
LOOK AT THE STARS
Atlantic #1144
Personal Management
James A. Dailey
1288 Madison Ave.
New York, New York
exclusively
ATLANTIC
records
Thanks DJs for all those spins

Jay's funniest gimmick, however, was beginning his act emerging from a coffin, a routine prompting more than one observer to dub him a 'black Vincent Price'. It hardly needs saying that during one performance his finger slipped when easing open the lid, causing it to get stuck - to much hilarity.

Jay's energy and obvious fitness belied that fact that he loved to drink. In fact, when we were with him he seemed to find it difficult to go on stage without a healthy fix of alcohol beforehand. One morning at the Uptown he appeared very agitated ahead of our 2pm show. He was constantly running around and kept disappearing for long intervals, only to reappear sweating profusely and highly stressed. It turned out that the local liquor stores didn't open before midday, not leaving him much time to source his booze, tank himself up and get changed into his weirdo garb ahead of the sound check and final rehearsal.

I bumped into Jay years later on the sidewalk in Manhattan, somewhere near Times Square, long after I had quit the music business. He was unmissable in his trademark headwear, which was somewhere between a low black top hat and a high pork pie. To his credit, he recognized me immediately. The guy had real style and always managed to behave like a true gentleman, despite living on the edge. Even though Jay went on to influence wild and weird performers in the late Sixties, such as Arthur Brown and Alice Cooper, to this day there still hasn't been anyone as original and way out as him.

******

One of the reasons Philly became such a favorite was because our success had at that point started to bring girls to the stage door. A lot of girls. Our time at the Uptown seemed to mark a step change in stage door hysteria for us and – what a surprise – we loved it!

Screamin' Jay Hawkins in his spooky stage outfit

The adulation would start with some pointing and giggling, then a little screaming and eventually some pushing and shoving as the girls became determined to make physical contact. One particular ritual happened after every performance, possibly because it involved the same girls every time. They would always grab Bobby by the neck, maybe as the surest way to drag his face downwards for a kiss. He was an obvious focal point for the fans because he was more often than not the lead singer. Bobby would pretend to resist a few times, before submitting to his tormentors. He didn't look at all tormented. Within a few minutes the dragging charade would become a kiss-fest involving all five of us. This was no great hardship. I know it seems like a ridiculous and meaningless thing to say, but I'll say it anyway: Philly girls were the best looking girls we ever saw on tour and we were sorry to leave after a week, knowing that the Uptown's stage door would be hard to match in theaters elsewhere.

Philly's apparent enthusiasm for the Mello-Kings seemed at odds with an item I stumbled across when leaving the Uptown one night. It was a wooden framed poster of the group that had been left out with the garbage at the back of the theatre. I could have interpreted this as a metaphor for the fragility of fame, but I rescued the picture and took it back to the house. I still have it to this day.

Chapter 6

American Bandstand

THE Holy Grail of media bookings for young pop stars in 1957 was *American Bandstand.* Unlike the Ed Sullivan Show, which presented variety acts alongside established singers and was aimed at a generally older audience, *Bandstand* was developed for showcasing the hottest new acts and targeted towards young people – effectively the buyers of those acts' records.

We were one of the first singing groups to appear on the show in its then new format. Premiered locally in 1952 as simply *Bandstand* on Philadelphia TV station WFIL-TV Channel 6, the show was picked up nationally by ABC, becoming *American Bandstand* on August 5, 1957. This first national broadcast of *American Bandstand* was filmed in the Starlight Ballroom in Wildwood NJ. Dick Clark, the host since 1956, stayed with the show for more than 30 years as it became a vehicle for his broad and lucrative entertainment career. Like us, he was a Mount Vernon guy; like me, he was an A.B. Davis High School guy.

Dick Clark probably wasn't thinking too much about the Mount Vernon connection when he personally called Al Silver to book us on to the show. Sales of *Tonite, Tonite* had already begun to gather pace in August 1957 and we were getting a lot of airplay. The fan base was growing fast. Al told us what we would get paid for the short TV appearance – a very respectable $362 between us, with no cut for him (he was delighted with the continued publicity for the record) - and a week later we gathered ourselves for the two hour drive to Philadelphia.

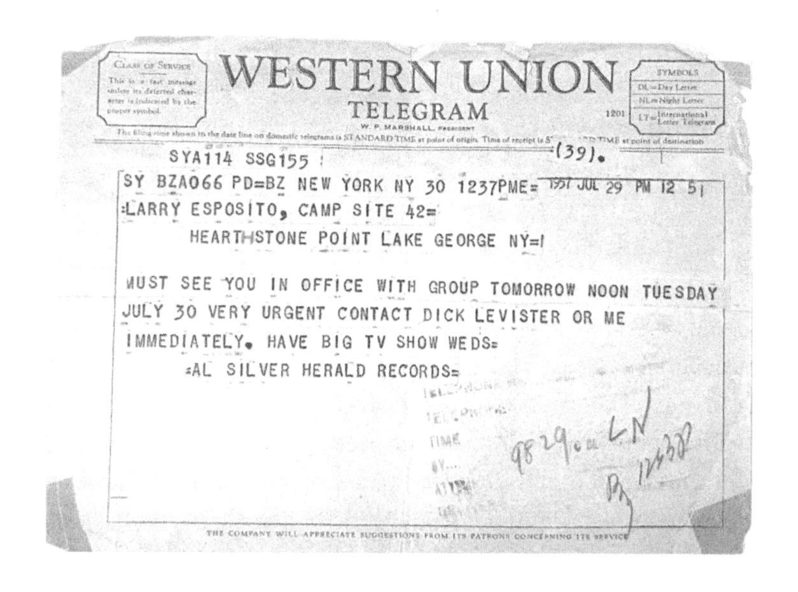
WESTERN UNION
TELEGRAM

SYA114 SSG155 (39).
SY BZA066 PD=BZ NEW YORK NY 30 1237PME= 1957 JUL 29 PM 12 51
=LARRY ESPOSITO, CAMP SITE 42=
HEARTHSTONE POINT LAKE GEORGE NY=

MUST SEE YOU IN OFFICE WITH GROUP TOMORROW NOON TUESDAY JULY 30 VERY URGENT CONTACT DICK LEVISTER OR ME IMMEDIATELY. HAVE BIG TV SHOW WEDS=
=AL SILVER HERALD RECORDS=

THE COMPANY WILL APPRECIATE SUGGESTIONS FROM ITS PATRONS CONCERNING ITS SERVICE

By this time we had a self-appointed 'official' driver, a skinny young Spanish guy named Chico Soto whom we knew from around Mount Vernon. Chico was about Larry's age, perhaps a little older, and seemed to have a great deal of spare time to hang out with us, which he enjoyed very much. When he wasn't driving or hanging, Chico would disappear for a while to work various jobs but would always make himself available to transport us to performances in his beloved red and white Ford. He was a great driver and rarely got lost, considering he didn't really know where he was going and GPS navigation was more than 40 years away.

Arriving in Philly a little early for the show, we were stretching our legs on the sidewalk after the ride when a group of four Hispanic girls strolled past us, giggling.

"Lots of handsome boys!" commented the 'leader' of the girls in Spanish. Chico overheard them.

"Yes, they certainly are," replied Chico, laughing. While I can't pretend this happened all the time, it was a fairly regular occurrence and our driver always accepted the compliments on our behalf with good grace.

WFIL's studio at 4548 Market Street, West Philadelphia, is said to have been the first purpose-built TV broadcast venue in the US. Studio B, home of *Bandstand*, was a vast space of more than 3,000 square feet and one side of it was pressed up against the Philadelphia Arena, the city's main sports venue. When we arrived there, the place was buzzing with organised chaos. We could see from our side entrance that the bleachers were already almost full and teenage kids were queueing either to reach their seats or to be told where to stand, ready to dance. The atmosphere of expectation was building, soundtracked by excited chatter. Older men were messing around with huge TV cameras attached to thick, snaking floor cables. Every so often one of a group of well presented, efficient-looking ladies would click past on high heels, striding purposefully toward the next task, reinforcing the divide between the kids and the grown-ups in the studio. Which were we? Although the same age as most of the audience, we were firmly part of the fast growing industry based on relieving these 15 year olds of their pocket money.

At the same time, a lot of the kids lined up to dance were dressed like their parents, especially the guys: sport coat and tie, a few with bow ties; some even with suits. Occasionally a pair of saddle shoes would jazz up an otherwise somewhat nerdy outfit. This aspect of *Bandstand*'s look and feel only underlined the show's 'whiteness' in its earlier TV days. I can't remember many, if any, black kids either dancing or in the audience when we went to the studio. There was no conscious segregation and Dick Clark seemed keen to run a more integrated show as the years went on; it's just something I thought about when looking back on this part of our journey.

"Let me show you how to get to Dick's office," said one of the clicking ladies when she spotted us in the corner, looking clueless. We followed her to a small room where Dick Clark was sitting on the edge of a desk that, unlike Al Silver, he obviously never worked behind. Smiling just enough to sweeten his business-like greeting, Dick Clark simply said: "Welcome, guys. Here's a copy of the show. You'll be lip-synching to your number – I hope that's OK?"

This matter-of-fact style of question was typical of Dick Clark. Don't get me wrong: he was a very nice guy, extremely pleasant; but a little serious for his 27 years and his personality wasn't huge, by any means. In those early days of televised *Bandstand*, always dressed in a conservative, gray flannel suit and dark tie, with hair perfectly slicked into place, Clark was frankly a little square for rock 'n' roll. In another life he would have continued relatively quietly with the radio career he'd always wanted to pursue, but I guess Alan Freed's success had opened his eyes to new possibilities and the potential of TV was beginning to explode. Now his eyes were firmly on the prize. That afternoon in the studio, Dick Clark's interaction with the kids while on screen was friendly and relaxed, but he remained reluctant to share their excitement, even when introducing the acts, and he was most definitely on the side of the 'grown-ups'. As I tracked Clark's career in the years that followed, I think it's fair to say that he loosened up a lot and grew into the role of TV host. In some ways, the role and its importance in broadcasting grew with him over the decades.

Dick Clark hosting American Bandstand, 1957

In answer to Dick Clark's question, no, we weren't necessarily OK with lip-synching, but we had little choice. It was what it was. While this wasn't an issue of 'artistic integrity', miming was alien to us and we were naturally very nervous about doing something totally new on one of America's biggest TV shows. Luckily, we weren't required to mime in silence: the idea was for us to sing normally, just over our own song; the studio audience would hear us singing along to *Tonite, Tonite*, but viewers at home would only hear the original track as recorded.

We got changed in a corner of Dick Clark's office when he left the room – there was no superstar treatment – and waited until we were called to take our positions: one microphone stand had been set up in a cleared space at floor level for Bobby and a second for the rest of us to share. A single camera would focus on the whole group.

It was a long wait before we were called. In those earlier days of TV advertising and program sponsorship, shows such as *Bandstand* made for very disjointed viewing as hosts were diverted from their main task every few minutes to make reference to an unrelated product or business. Even the opening credits, during which couples were shown jiving as Charles Albertine's *Bandstand Boogie* played, Dick Clark's voice would announce: "American Bandstand, brought to you by crystal clear 7-Up! A fresh clean taste – nothing does it quite like 7-Up, that's for sure!" Strangely, it was during these plugs that Dick Clark was at his most animated and enthusiastic, even entering into dialogue with audience members close to his 'presenting desk' who begged to try some of the advertiser's soda, or candy or whatever. Sure enough, several commercial pauses occurred as we continued to hang around, now changed into in our group outfits, close to Dick Clark's office. It was an opportunity to check out the cute girls in the studio – and there were a lot of them. Man, I thought those Philly girls were quite something! Of course, there was no real reason why the young females two hours' drive from home should be any prettier than those in Mount Vernon. I guess I was caught up in the moment and feeling cuter than usual myself.

Like many young guys watching the show at the time, I had eyes for two very different regular dancers on Bandstand. Carole Scaldeferri was 15 when we appeared on the show. Brunette and Italian like me, I heard she used to bring a change of clothes to the studio so that she never had to appear on set in her Catholic School uniform. Carole's dance partner, Harvey Robbins, was equally popular with girl viewers. Justine Carrelli, by contrast, was very blonde and became better known, not least for her 'are they or aren't they' relationship with dance partner Bob Clayton. Only 13 when she first graced the studio, Justine had to borrow both her sister's birth certificate and black eye make-up to satisfy the over-14s-only rule. The boys and I managed to get a closer look at Justine on our second visit to *Bandstand.*

When we were beginning to wonder if the show's sponsor must surely have run out of contractual plugs, we were finally ushered towards our microphones and, with a cheery but basic introduction from Dick Clark, the recording of *Tonite, Tonite* began to play. All credit to Bobby for being counted in to the song 'blind' because, as fans of the record will know only too well, there is no musical intro: the first three notes are Bobby, unaccompanied, singing "*To-oo-ooo...*" before the drums, bass and piano join on "*nite*". Once we knew that Bobby's live voice, audible to the studio crowd, had synched to the intro, all was good and we sang our hearts out as if there were no backing track at all.

Justine Carrelli and Bob Clayton, popular Bandstand dancers

The audience loved us. They weren't quite screaming, but the applause was loud and enthusiastic, especially from the girls in the bleachers, and there had been lots of ooh-ing and ahh-ing during the song. Dick Clark got up from behind his presenting desk to greet us at our microphones.

"Wow, boys, looks like you were a hit," he said, grinning while also refraining from fulsome praise. Our song was already gaining popularity and almost certainly known to many of the kids there, but few had seen us until then, unless they had been to one of our smaller gigs further north. We were still being presented as a new act – at least on TV. To put it in context, the day before we had appeared on the show, Andy Williams had stood in the same spot. Two days after us, one of my own heroes, Tony Bennett, would sing there. Fats Domino the day after that. "Who do we have here, then? What are your names?" continued our host, thrusting his own microphone into Bobby's face, amid much giggling and whispering in the audience, and working his way through the group. Dick Clark repeated each name in turn. When he came to me and I said "Neil," he just nodded. I didn't take it personally, but we laughed later when I got fan mail addressed to 'the other one' from girls who'd watched the show and picked out their favourite Mello-King.

None of us was in any doubt that our *Bandstand* debut had been a great success and Dick Clark seemed happy that he'd booked us. So happy, in fact, that he said he had a proposition for us, if we'd hang around for a bit after the show.

******

Calmly pleased with himself, Clark swung by the back of the studio at around 4.30pm to find us waiting patiently. "I wanted to talk to you about something: I have a sock hop in Wildwood this evening, but I have no-one to perform. You guys should come along, sing *a capella* - it'll be fun. I'll give you money for gas." He gave Chico $20 and we all looked at each other. There wasn't much to say. "OK?" Clark checked. Some nodding all round and we got into Chico's Ford, three in the front, three in the back. Clark climbed into a regular sedan which he drove himself, nothing fancy, and we followed him to the southern end of the New Jersey coast, like cops trailing a criminal.

Wildwood wasn't exactly on the way home and while Chico may have been happy cruising with his gas paid, the rest of us were still unclear about what was going on. Even so, arriving in the resort city at around 6pm that day didn't feel like a terrible hardship. It was, and still is, a really fun place and, in 1957, a center of youth culture and music with wide, sandy beaches, thrill rides and diners. Now, the resort's Fox Park is home to the Doo Wop Experience museum, crammed with 1950s memorabilia. We may even be in there, somewhere.

Strolling aimlessly up and down the long boardwalk, four of five guys passed us, then one turned around and yelled, "Hey, aren't you guys the Mello-Kings?"

"Yeah, we are."

"We just saw you on Bandstand! You guys are cool, man!"

"Thanks!"

It put a bit more of a spring in our step as we continued to promenade. Music played constantly from the eateries and stands. The hits of the day were adding to the sense of excitement building as young people flocked to Wildwood for the late summer evening, older visitors going home and making way for teens on dates, or at least hoping to meet a new one. Out of the five of us, Eddie and I were by far the most 'into' music and September 1957 was a vintage month for the Billboard charts. We were loving the variety of great numbers, not just R&B and doo-wop, but ballads, rock 'n' roll and the unclassifiable other stuff that was just great pop. To give you an idea, this was the top of the chart in that first weekend of September 1957:

1. Debbie Reynolds -Tammy
2. Paul Anka - Diana
3. Elvis Presley - (Let Me Be Your) Teddy Bear
4. The Crickets -That'll Be the Day
5. The Everly Brothers - Bye Bye Love
6. Jerry Lee Lewis -Whole Lot of Shakin'
7. Russ Hamilton - Rainbow
8. Jimmie Rodgers - Honeycomb
9. Pat Boone - Love Letters in the Sand
10. The Coasters - Searchin'.

You can see that the bar was high for young artists like us: at least half of that list alone became all-time classics.

Our performance space was outdoors, with a stage and a canopy. Dick Clark was working these events regularly at the time, trying to maintain Jersey interest in his various music enterprises. That night, there must have been close to 1,000 kids in the audience.

Taking the microphone and gazing over this small sea of teenagers, Dick Clark announced: "Hey everybody, you might have been lucky enough to catch the Mello-Kings with me on the show earlier. Well, I've brought them with me to Wildwood tonight! Here they are, the Mello-Kings!" We did three or four numbers, including *Tonite, Tonite* and *Do Baby Do*. The crowd had been warmed up by a DJ spinning the latest discs and seemed to be having a great time. Many had indeed seen us earlier – such was the huge popularity of *Bandstand* in those eastern states – and watching us sing without a band didn't dampen their enthusiasm one bit. Dick Clark disappeared into thin air from the moment the lights were fixed on us. We didn't see him again that night.

******

We got back to Mount Vernon way after midnight. It was Wednesday morning. Our first appearance on *Bandstand* had been on a Tuesday afternoon and our unscheduled trip to Wildwood left us three-and-a-half hours from home. On a schoolnight. This last fact was increasingly irrelevant, as rock‘n’roll had effectively put us (except Larry) on a hiatus from school. I can only speak for my own circumstances, which had involved a great deal of forebearance from school, where – partly because of my value to A.B. Davis as a basketball player – most teachers were remarkably understanding, indeed very supportive of my musical career.

This is how it worked for me. By the time our second appearance on *Bandstand* was looming, I had already missed a ton of school. My report card screamed in bright red: “50! Incomplete status!”. Mom was getting calls from school about my lack of attendance and, although she was supportive and helping me to get away with not being present while I lived the rock‘n’roll dream, it was beginning to turn into a big, unaddressed problem. When I eventually found myself back in class for a few days, I was told to report to the Dean of Boys, Maurice Childs. There were two issues he wanted to address. First, a number of teachers had complained I was setting a bad example to younger students by holding Mary Ann’s hand in the hallways and kissing her goodbye before we headed into our classes. Miss Stiles, the French teacher, had also seen us from her fourth floor window, kissing in the school grounds. When she started tapping loudly on the window and wagging ‘no-no’ with her finger, we turned to look up and just burst out laughing. Secondly, I was to receive a formal warning that I would be expelled from school if my non-attendance continued.

Dean Childs was very old and unthreatening. Balding with big ears, he looked a little like Benjamin Franklin after a severe haircut.

"So, Neil, a lot of the teachers are complaining about how affectionate you are in the hallway with your girlfriend."

"Dean Childs, I'm in love," was my unflinching return of his opening serve.

"OK. What if Mrs Childs and I arrived in the parking lot, here at school in the morning, and she wanted to kiss me goodbye to wish me a good day? How would that look in front of everybody?"

"Dean Childs, I saw that happen once and I thought it was really cute."

"No, no, you're missing the point." He was starting, in his quiet way, to get exasperated. This wasn't going to be as straightforward as he'd hoped. "Sometimes these things just aren't appropriate. Do you see?"

I looked at him, smiling faintly, as if to show I was following him, but with a look that suggested I hadn't a clue what the next move in this game might be.

He gave up. Instead of sighing he just nodded repeatedly and breathed out through his nose in a pronounced way. On to the next part.

"Neil, let's be honest about your commitment to school. In the last 45 days you've attended 15 times. I can't have that. What are you going to do? At some point you have to make a choice between school and a musical career. What's it going to be?"

"Dean Childs, at this time I have no idea. I'm having a good time with the music business right now. I can't think further than our next appearance. By the way, we've been invited back on *American Bandstand*."

End of difficult conversation. I had pressed the correct button. Dean Childs wasn't a natural *Bandstand* viewer, but his enthusiasm was fuelled by Dick Clark being a Davis alumnus. He had also personally taught Clark, of whom he was clearly a big fan.

Dean Childs

And Clark was a big fan of Dean Childs, remembering him very fondly. I was given a letter from Childs to pass on to Clark, which I put together with a book for signing, from Miss Dorothy Feaster, an ancient, white haired teacher in the English department and a formidable A.B. Davis veteran. "Ah yes, good ol' Dean Childs," said Clark when I shared these with him, "and is 'she' still there?" referring to Miss Feaster.

All in all, despite going through the motions to remind me I was ultimately still a schoolkid, most teachers were on my side. They and a lot of the A.B. Davis students had seen us on TV with Dick Clark before. Now, ahead of our second appearance, the school's collective excitement had reached the daily bulletin, in which Dean Childs had urged, "Don't forget to tune into *American Bandstand* to watch our own Neil Arena!"

******

Within a few days of our return from Wildwood, Dick Levister took a call from Al Silver.

"I've got three big sacks of mail for your boys. Someone needs to come and get them out of my office." *Bandstand* had won us a lot of new fans and the performance had moved them to write us, with Herald Records being the only obvious mailing address.

"Dear Mello-Kings, I hope you get this letter. I loved your song on *American Bandstand* – you were great. Enclosed is $5. Please send an autographed photograph."

Since Levister didn't drive and this wasn't an appealing favor to ask Chico, because the group wouldn't be there, we enlisted the help of Bobby Solano's brother, Quentin, to fetch our letters from Broadway. There were literally hundreds of envelopes and the mail sacks would have been far too heavy for Levister to lift on his own, even if he'd had his own wheels. When we read them later that day, we were on cloud nine. It was the coolest thing ever. We decided we would have to get a bunch of 3x5 photographs printed to meet this new demand - one of many things we ended up paying for ourselves. Mysteriously, very few of the letters had any cash with them by the time they reached us in Mount Vernon.

******

Our second *Bandstand* appearance was only six weeks later on Wednesday October 16, 1957. Again, we were the only group singing in the studio (often there were two) but the format of the show was slightly different, with a segment that involved a panel of teens voting on the songs they heard. Since we were last on the show, *Tonite, Tonite* had gained momentum in both sales and airplay. We had toured extensively and it's fair to say that we had become well known very quickly, which was reflected in the very different reception we got from the bleachers crowd the second time. There was loud applause ahead of us taking our places at the microphones and some of the girls were calling out our names.

Now unfazed by lip-synching, although it remained something we only did on *Bandstand*, we settled down to treat our new Philly friends to *Sassafrass*. The guys and I were relaxed and moving to the music as the recorded intro began: less than 10 seconds of Leroy Kirkland playing an upbeat, bluesy guitar lick. Even I enjoyed singing my least favourite Mello-Kings number that afternoon, feeling confident and admired by the crowd, who seemed to be rocking with us. The reaction when we'd finished was also positive, so we were surprised when the panel of three random kids, feeding their view back to Dick Clark, only awarded the song 62 points out of 100.

"Shame, the Mello-Kings are going to be disappointed," said Clark.

Their reasoning was that they thought it was difficult to dance to. We found that hard to believe, since every night dancers attending the show were developing new moves to go with all kinds of records. It was part of what *Bandstand* was about and our song hadn't troubled those couples on the floor too much when we were singing. But on that afternoon, the geeky young guy and the two girls with him in the studio became what the media these days call 'opinion formers' or 'influencers'. Shooting down our song, they were shaping the perception of the viewers at home and, sure enough, sales of the single bombed. Damned by three kids.

Thank God we had been invited to sing two songs. *Chapel on the Hill*, the flip side of the disc, had us back in more comfortable ballad territory and the girls in the crowd were swooning once again. They particularly liked the gentle 'Ding Dong' harmonised vocal ending I had devised for us, which ended with an oboe flourish. Sadly, the panel hadn't been asked to rate *Chapel*, which I still think is our finest performance on record.

After the show, a little stall with a table had been set up for us to sign autographs. I found myself manning this station on my own, since the boys had dispersed to talk to fans and had forgotten to follow me. To my absolute delight, Justine sauntered over by herself. She was carrying what must have been an autograph book, by then already full of names much more famous than ours. I thought to myself: "Oh my God, she's gorgeous. I have to ask her for her number." She smiled as she handed me the book. Giving it back, after being careful to look cool and grown-up while signing it, I said: "Thanks for coming over."

"You're welcome – I loved the song," she replied. At that moment, at least, her opinion mattered way more than getting even a 62 from the panel of idiots. Getting her number would have been even better.

The '62' bump in our otherwise smooth road to date only confirmed what we had thought in earlier weeks: Herald had messed up by pushing *Sassafrass* instead of *Chapel*. It turned out to be a missed opportunity for both us and the record company. Still, it seemed to have no effect on bookings from promoters who were crazy for groups hot from *Bandstand* and we were straight back on the road.

Chapter 7

A Whole Lotta Shakin' with the Hound Dog

WHILE the 'Chitlin' Circuit' was the go-to theater tour for black R&B acts, a little further north in the east coast states another George was launching his own important platform for popular artists.

Rock and roll had many founding fathers, but high up on the list has to be George Lorenz. When we met George in 1957 he was in his late 30s and hosting a very popular radio show from WKBW, Buffalo, NY. He was nicknamed the 'Hound Dog', nothing to do with Elvis's hit the previous year with a Big Mama Thornton song of the same name, but after a 1940s expression, 'doggin' around', meaning messing about or hanging around. He'd open his show by saying "Here I am to dog around for another hour." George loved this beat or jive slang which wasn't necessarily cool to his listeners 20-plus years younger, but worked well when delivered in his rich, soft voice as he introduced the latest wax from Jerry Lee Lewis or Chuck Berry. Those who had never seen Hound Dog might have been surprised at pictures of a favourite uncle with a confused fashion sense: a short guy of about 5'6", slicked back prematurely greying hair, longish sideburns and a goatee beard which often sat atop a thin bow tie. A slight limp made him waddle.

WKBW was a great base from which to spread the gospel of rock and roll. The station was heard in 20 states, as well as in Canada, an audience big enough for George to launch his own weekly Top 10 newsletter. It was natural for the Hound Dog Show to progress to live DJ performances in clubs, then on to booking artists for concert tours and November 1957 saw George take an Eighth Anniversary Show of Stars around the north east states: Rochester NY, Scranton PA, Providence RI and Hartford CT. Touring alongside the Mello-Kings were the Billy Williams Quartet, Roy Hamilton, the Tune Weavers, Little Joe, The Bobbettes, The Clovers, Thurston Harris, Doc Bagby and our old friend Screamin' Jay Hawkins. It was a fun line up with a mix of youngsters and more seasoned performers, but the shorter 'advance' tour beginning in the station's home city of Buffalo on 24 October was another affair altogether, since it was headlined by the legendary Jerry Lee Lewis.

In case you're hoping for tales of joshing with Jerry Lee on the tour bus, I have to disappoint you from the off. The superstar always drove himself, with his 'band' of drummer and electric bass player following – two redheaded guys who never seemed to speak and just did what they were told. Joining us on the bus were Thurston, Little Joe, Roy and the Chantels. It may have seemed like a tame bunch, but we still managed to have a great time. The Mello-Kings would entertain the others while practising their modern harmony routine. Roy, especially, loved our version of *Moonlight in Vermont*. He was always a great supporter of ours. Eddie usually sat next to me and he'd tease me mercilessly when my head would drop on to his shoulder as I fell asleep, dribbling and snoring. "Hey Funk Breath! Put your head the other way!"

The slightly older guys might have wondered what they were doing riding with a bunch of kids and neither was a wild rock and

George 'Hound Dog' Lorenz

roller. Thurston was around 26, a laid-back tall, slim black guy with smiling but slightly sleepy eyes. He was unfailingly polite and chilled around us immature teenagers. Originally from Indianapolis, Thurston had only recently gone solo, having spent the previous four years with Los Angeles based vocal group the Lamplighters, who had also worked with the famed blues-shouter Jimmy Witherspoon. Now signed to LA's Aladdin Records and backed by his original group, renamed the Sharps, he was touring on the back of a Top Ten national hit and million seller, a cover of Bobby Day's *Little Bitty Pretty One*. It was a great song and Thurston's version has been featured in many movies over the decades.

Little Joe – a relative geriatric at 34 – couldn't have been more different. He was possibly as 'Little' as five feet, or at least that was how small he seemed to me. Remember, I was still only about 5'7" at the time, while Eddie and Jerry weren't much bigger, yet we towered over Joe. A Philadelphian with a gospel singing background, Joe had decided to migrate his trademark falsetto to the world of doo-wop, leading a group called the Thrillers and signing to R&B label Okeh. The group's second single, *Peanuts,* charted just before the Hound Dog tour and reached #22. I didn't know until I saw the label many years later that the orchestral arrangement on *Peanuts* was by our own arranger Leroy Kirkland. Joe's high register on the song is thought to have influenced Frankie Valli who, of course, covered *Tonite, Tonite*. Every night, on both the Jerry Lee leg of the tour and the main Hound Dog Anniversary dates, Joe would be sure to call his beloved young family back home. "Tell Mommy that Daddy's selling peanuts," he would always say to whichever of his many kids had picked up the phone. His wife was always too busy to talk.

******

To say the tour dates were plugged on Hound Dog's show for weeks before would be a gross understatement. By 24 October it seemed as if not a single person in Buffalo didn't know that Jerry Lee Lewis would be playing the Memorial Auditorium – 'the Aud' – supported by a long cast of popular acts. In truth, the only performer with a fan base even beginning to approach Jerry Lee's was Jay Hawkins, but even then it was a long drop down on the bill from one wild man of rock and roll to the other; it was a big drop yet again to the rest of the acts. Nonetheless, everyone else performing had enjoyed recording success, multiple TV appearances and gained several thousand followers in the months leading up to the Hound Dog tour.

The idea was that Jerry Lee would play Buffalo, Rochester and Scranton on consecutive nights. You might ask if the Catholic Youth Center in Scranton was quite ready to host a man with a hell-raising reputation who, within a few months, would marry his 13 year old cousin. The answer is probably not, given that 'The Killer' was, in 1957, just about the most controversial and outrageous performer to play anywhere in the US – with the possible exception of Little Richard. The star was then scheduled to leave us to appear on the Steve Allen Show and then on Bandstand, while the rest of us started again in Rochester.

Located in downtown Buffalo, near the walkway alongside the Niagara River, the Aud opened in the early 1940s as a sporting arena. It seated 12,000 for ice hockey and up to another 3,000 in the floor area for basketball - it was home to the Canisius Golden Griffins. The 'Memorial' part of the auditorium's name came from its dedication to those who had lost their lives in World War 1. In the early Fifties it also grew in importance as a concert venue and in 1957 the Aud's most notable gig before ours with Jerry Lee was Elvis Presley's last performance before his two years in the army.

The Mello-Kings opened all the multi-artist shows in both 'halves' of the Hound Dog tour. Sure, we were among the smaller acts compared to Jay Hawkins and Jerry Lee, but we were also great openers: energetic, fun and possibly better at getting the party started than a girl group or solo act. Bear in mind that the audience was hyper and full of expectation, thousands of kids already drunk on the atmosphere, so the show needed to go off with a bang. It was Hound Dog's tour so, unsurprisingly, he was the MC for every gig. Duck-like, he walked to the center of the stage and began to welcome everyone. It's at this point that the first act has to wait in the wings listening to a preamble that seems endless, wondering

HOUND DOG'S
GREAT IN PERSON GREAT
ANNIVERSARY SHOW
ALL IN PERSON
ALL IN PERSON
The Billy WILLIAMS Quartet
Jerry Lee LEWIS
"WHOLE LOT OF SHAKIN' GOING ON"
Roy HAMILTON
The MELLO-KINGS
The TUNE WEAVERS
Little JOE
The BOBBETTES
MR. LEE
The LOVERS
ALL IN PERSON
The CLOVERS
DOWN IN THE ALLEY
JAY HAWKINS
Thurston HARRIS
Duke JENKINS and Orch.
"DOC" BAGBY
ALL IN PERSON
ALL IN PERSON
GEORGE "HOUND DOG" LORENZ of WKBW, M.C.
ONE NITE ONLY
C.Y.C. (Scranton), Thurs., Oct. 31 8:30 P.M.
SEATS $1.75 — $2.00 — $2.50 — $3.00
Now on Sale at Spruce Record, Reismans, Record Rack, Adams Malt, Perry's Record (Carbondale), Pittston Record (Pittston), Square Record and Green's Card (Wilkes-Barre).

nervously when the subject will suddenly swing to them or their group. That lurch in the chat was usually, for me, accompanied by my heartrate spiking and I'd be like a coiled spring, ready to be released into the auditorium.

"Now it's my pleasure to introduce our wonderful opening act, the Mello-Kings!" George Lorenz extended his arm and turned not quite half way behind as I ran on, followed by the others. I was quite overwhelmed when I saw the size of the crowd. It didn't seem to end. I think I'd have crapped my pants if I'd been standing there alone. They wouldn't stop applauding for maybe another whole minute. All we could do was keep staring ahead, waiting until they'd finished. What happened next did nothing to calm my nerves. After waiting for what seemed like 10 silent seconds for the band to start the intro for our first number, *Do Baby Do*. The noise in the arena died down to allow the band to start playing, but when they did it was all wrong. Already an uptempo number, the idiots had made the intro possibly three times faster. We simply couldn't keep up to jump in at the right time. Hound Dog looked on from the wings as we shuffled nervously while shooting daggers at the bandleader and trying to signal that there had been a terrible mistake. They realized just in time, before it became too obvious from playing an insanely fast and repetitive intro, and simply started again.

Tonite, Tonite was harder for them to mess up, because of its *a capella* intro. By the time we'd finished, the crowd had forgotten our inauspicious start and we had them eating out of our hands. Lorenz was highly satisfied and patted each of our backs as we jogged offstage, telling us we'd handled the early confusion very well.

Actually, it was in Buffalo that I almost came to perform a second time in one night with a different group. The Tune Weavers were a mixed four-piece vocal group in their early 20s, a curious

The Tune Weavers

combination of folk, doo-wop, jazz and R&B, comprising husband-and-wife team Margo and John Sylvia, Margo's brother Gil and her cousin Charlotte. They had just enjoyed a #5 Billboard hit with Margo and Gil's song *Happy, Happy Birthday Baby*, a slow, romantic number with beautiful harmonies, which to be honest I found a little plodding. Bass singer John was feeling unwell as the group was set to go onstage. Aware of the Mello-Kings' harmonies and having seen us open the show, I was scouted as a last-minute replacement, in the spirit of 'The Show Must Go On!'. Luckily for all of us, John managed to pull himself together just in time to go on stage. I'm sure I would have done '*Happy Birthday'* justice and the Tune Weavers were a really nice bunch, but I was pleased to stay in the wings for their set.

These 'package' shows were great value for the audience, which was royally entertained for at least a couple of hours in total, with each act performing two or three songs. We had played the same bill as Billy Williams before, as well as Roy Hamilton. New to us was Doc Bagby, an old-school jazzer of around 40 who had crossed over to rock and roll with his piano and organ. Among his many songwriting credits was *Rock the Joint*, a big hit for Bill Haley. We also enjoyed The Lovers, the husband-and-wife duo of Allen Bunn and Anna Sandford. They were in the charts at the time with a cute little R&B track, *Darling It's Wonderful*. There was huge variety overall and, later on the bill, Jay Hawkins didn't disappoint as he treated the crowd to his inimitable lunacy. Of course, only one performer in Buffalo that night could upstage Jay.

******

To this day, Jerry Lee Lewis remains one of the top five artists that shaped rock and roll in the Fifties and continued to influence performers for half a century afterwards. He's up there with Elvis, Chuck Berry, Little Richard and Buddy Holly. Much has been written about Jerry Lee's backstory and his journey to stardom, so I'll just give you my personal take on the guy, which I gained at close quarters. To my mind, looking beyond R&B, doo-wop and the more 'mainstream' male singers that launched their careers at that time, Jerry Lee Lewis was the true definition of a Fifties rock star: unrefined, outrageous, controversial, raunchy – and wildly entertaining. Elvis had gyrated his way into young girls' hearts, but their moms would have probably loved him too; Buddy was a clean cut pop artist, rather than a rock and roller; Little Richard was eccentric and off-the-scale crazy, but fun. Jerry Lee, however, spelled danger. In quiet mode, there was an arrogance and stand-offishness about him. He seemed unapproachable and dark. While the young Mello-Kings didn't want to risk prodding the bear and invading the privacy of his dressing room in Buffalo, we still tried to engage with him several times in the course of our short tour together to see if he was capable of lightening up. "Hey, Killer!" we'd call out as he walked past us, hoping for a wink or some other sort of friendly reply. "Hey Jerry Lee, how's it goin'?" Nothing. He completely ignored us. If he was sitting in his room he'd always be fussing with his clothes or string in the mirror.

Walking on to that stage in Buffalo, he was all smiles, but his eyes remained steely. Tall for those times, maybe nearly six feet, so definitely above average, his lean frame loped towards the piano to get straight down to business. No niceties or messing about. No sooner had his butt touched the stool that he attacked the keyboard with the stabbing four rising chords that introduced his new song, *Great Balls of Fire.*

"You shake my nerves and you rattle my brain!" he howled in his powerful, wavering voice, before the next four stabs. Sitting at 45 degrees facing the audience while he sang, his right leg semi-draped across the side of the stool, he tapped his foot casually as if listening to someone else's record. *"Kiss me ba-by! Mmmm, feels GOOD!"* he continued, eyes darting back and forth throughout this sassy delivery. Jerry Lee's blond hair, thick and wavy like crinkle-cut fries, began the song perfectly in place above his flattish, rather triangular face. Within seconds, his helmet had started to unfurl, ringlets dangling over his ears as he sweated, shook and wrestled with the piano. There was no doubt that this was technically a percussion instrument: pounding the keys wasn't enough; he was beating the shit out of them. I wondered if they'd still be white by the time he'd finished his next number, *Whole Lotta Shaking Goin'*

On, his earlier hit cover of Big Maybelle's song. Musically, however, Jerry Lee was undeniably impressive: for all the showmanship, his piano playing was very accurate, despite rarely glancing at his instrument; I also think his voice was overlooked – a well projected and note perfect tenor, even with his trademark sing-song intonation.

The Jerry Lee I saw in 1957 was manic when he played, his own songs giving him an adrenalin rush. Rock stars didn't start smashing guitars and kicking over drum kits at the end of their sets until at least 10 years later, but I wouldn't have been at all surprised if The Killer had kicked the hell out of his piano before walking off stage. Eddie and I were sure to catch his set every night from the wings, wondering if he'd eventually freak out and pull a crazy stunt. Legend has it that a few months later, while on an Alan Freed tour with a few of the same Buffalo acts, he set fire to his piano using oil he kept onstage in a Coke can. None of the other artists has ever said they saw it. Either way, you could say Jerry Lee Lewis was the very first punk rocker, two decades ahead of his time. In terms of sheer excitement, I have seen no other performer like him.

******

The Rochester Community War Memorial (now the Blue Cross Arena) was a brand new stadium built no more than two years before as a replacement for the Edgerton Park Arena. Both had served as the home of the Rochester Royals NBA basketball team. Seating 10,000-plus, it wasn't a mega-theatre for concerts, but still became a permanent fixture on later US tours for global acts such as the Rolling Stones and Led Zeppelin. They would have been relieved not to need backing musicians, especially those supporting the Hound Dog tour that night. After the usual introduction from

Jerry Lee Lewis, hair still in place

Lorenz himself, I ran out on stage first, as had become the Mello-Kings' routine. The applause was rapturous and, for the second night and in a different city, I felt almost physically blown over by the force of the enthusiastic reception. This crowd was really up for a good time! The others came running on, one by one, to a similar reaction until we were all in our respective places at the mics. We were much less nervous in Rochester and played a great set, the send-off from the crowd being even more appreciative than our welcome.

Not all the acts were able to join the tour for all eight nights – three with Jerry Lee and five without – despite appearing on the poster for each theater. Our old friends from Philly week, the Bobbettes, were unable to skip school for the whole run since they were, on average, still only 14. They were replaced on certain nights by the Chantels, only slightly older and about to become only the second (after the Bobbettes) African American girl group to achieve national success. Formed in a Catholic school in the Bronx, not a million miles from our own Mount Vernon base, the Chantels were a five-piece vocal act led by the classically trained Arlene Smith, who was also their main songwriter. Before the Hound Dog tour, their first single, *He's Gone*, had been a very minor hit in August. I thought it was a great song, showcasing beautifully the group's skilful harmonies as well as Arlene's powerful solo voice. She really was something else and it was hard to believe that such a force could be produced by the skinny little girl before our eyes. I mean, she was barely visible behind the mic stand!

Standing in for the Bobbettes meant covering their smash hit song Mr Lee. The Chantels' version was as at least as good as the original. They finished their set with the just recorded but not yet released *Maybe*, a piano-heavy number with rich harmonies overlaid by Arlene's expressive and soulful lead vocal. Magnificent.

******

There were no hotels involved on the Hound Dog tour, except for between the last two nights in Hartford on 7-8 November. We barely knew where we were going from one day to the next, joining the tour bus in the New York area every day and getting dropped back late at night after the show. Generally, we couldn't have even told you where we were headed when we got on. Bobby, however, clearly had a better grip of the tour's logistics when we finished playing our second visit to Rochester. Boarding the bus late after the show, we noticed a brunette we didn't recognize standing on the sidewalk just behind us – a very good looking chick with a hot body. She proceeded to lasso Bobby, who was walking towards the bus, lagging us by a few paces, and dragged him away (quite impressive since he and Larry were significantly taller than the other three Mello-Kings) bundling him into a car. Bobby was a willing victim in this abduction. There was very little resistance and both he and the girl couldn't stop laughing. We didn't know how to react: Jerry, as his kid brother, kind of trusted him to know what he was doing; Eddie, Larry and I were partly shocked, partly impressed. Like our 'nocturnal groupie' incident in Philly, this was rock and roll! Within a few minutes, however, our feelings had changed to panic. What if he didn't come back, at least in time for the next show? What would we say to Lorenz? Our career had reached new highs on that tour, but it could all be over.

I say that Bobby had a better sense of geography than his groupmates because he was driven by his kidnapper straight to Scranton the next day. He was proudly exhausted and probably couldn't wait for it to happen again – with a different girl.

There were always lots of girls chasing us and, by that time in autumn 1957, we were a very popular bunch of guys. But it was all pretty innocent stuff. Mostly. Only once was I in a potentially embarrassing situation when we played Hartford on the last night. My girlfriend Mary Ann had come to watch the final show, but there had been a girl on this overnighter who had been trying to get with me – and wanted to meet up with me at the end. Mary Ann was gorgeous and, weirdly, this other girl looked a lot like her; I suppose that's why she caught my eye. Anyway, disaster was averted and the three of us were never in the same place. It was particularly lucky because Mary Ann's dad was coming to drive us home from Hartford.

Alphonso Lieto (or Al to his friends) and his wife Grace had no other children. He was in the insurance business – a coincidence, since that would be my later career – and she was a homemaker. A heavy smoker, Grace sadly died of lung cancer, predeceasing her husband by some years. Al was a great supporter of mine, having also come to the Apollo to see me, so I would have hated to upset or disappoint him and his daughter. They were a lovely family and an important part of my formative years, however precociously successful I had become.

Chapter 8

My Kinda Town

I played alongside some great names in some huge venues during my time in the Mello-Kings, but a great favourite among tours, theaters and cities had to be Chicago. Irv Nahan had secured us a seven-day booking at the famous Regal in November 1957 and it was an experience I still treasure. Quite simply, it was one of the best times I ever had in the group.

The Windy City seemed a million miles away to us. In reality, it was 900 miles west of Mount Vernon; not an enormous distance by today's standards but, to be fair, I think it was the first time any of us had travelled to a different time zone. Our journey would take us more than 14 hours in the Mello-Bomb, but this time it was Levister driving, even though I wasn't sure he even had a license. It was our only whole day off between the Hound Dog tour and Regal week, so we would need all the rest we could get on the road before starting in Chicago on Friday 8 November. We met very early at Mom's Diner and saw him swing round the corner in the huge, ugly station-wagon. Its vast trunk was a blessing since it had to carry the luggage of six guys with several changes of clothes – we certainly never did any laundry on tour. Brothers Jerry and Bobby joined

Levister on the bench seat in front, while Larry, Eddie and I sat behind.

Sometimes we listened to the radio as we drove, lending our critical ears to the latest releases and, more often than not, agreeing that we could do better. This would then prompt us all to break into song, either fine tuning the harmonies for our touring repertoire, or developing new versions of our favourite classics: proper songs written for proper singers – Ella, Frank, Dean, Tony. I don't remember stopping for food even once on that long drive, although there must have been toilet breaks. However, an enforced stop eventually came in the form of a flat tire. All things considered, the old jalopy did us proud over its remaining life with us. We had got off very lightly, with no major repairs needed. The flat could've happened in a brand new car. It took a while to register with us, the Mello-Bomb being so overloaded with guys and bags, plus its barge-like bulk and long wheelbase made for a soft ride. It was only when one side of the car became noticeably lower and we heard a scraping sound that we knew something was up.

"Oh crap! Good thing we left a day early to get here," said Eddie, staring at the flattened rubber.

We were in the middle of nowhere on the relatively new I-80. Eddie and I set about changing the tire. Neither of us had taken shop at school - he hadn't been at A.B. Davis, but at Archbishop Stepanic, a Catholic school 30 minutes away in White Plains – but it really wasn't complicated, although Larry and the Scholls showed no inclination to help. Remembering this makes me wonder what would've happened if we hadn't had a spare. I was way more organized than the others: I'd brought $50 with me in case we all needed to get home by other means; they were terrible with money and generally didn't carry much, if any.

******

It was a very big deal to have landed a week at the Regal, for many reasons, not least because it cemented our standing as a *bona fide* R&B act – we were in a segment of the music industry comprising almost exclusively black artists. Not for the first time, we were to be the only white act on the bill and the others were top names on the Chitlin' Circuit: Titus Turner, Frankie Lee Sims, Mercy Baby, Big Maybelle, Priscilla Bowman, our old friend Screamin' Jay Hawkins and – most exciting of all – superstars The Dells. They were R&B royalty. Many were accompanied by the Al Smith 'Orchestra', a collection of jazzers who had turned to playing blues and soul, led by chubby bass player Al. Most of the artists were represented by Archer Associates, a major agency of the time led by talent supremo Jack Archer (no relation to George, whom we would meet later). The week's engagement was named 'Al Benson's Rock and Roll Show'. It had followed other teenage oriented package shows entitled 'Al Benson's Rhythm and Blues Show' and 'Al Benson's All New Rock and Roll Jamboree'.

Yes, of course I'm going to tell you about Al Benson! Essentially, Al was to Chicago what George Woods had been to Philadelphia: a DJ, promoter, civil rights activist and champion of black music on radio in that major city and far beyond. Originally from Mississippi like his regular collaborator Al Smith, he had also practised as an ordained minister under his real name, Arthur Leaner. Curiously, ministry had been his introduction to radio in the mid-Forties, broadcasting sermons and gospel music to Chicago's African American community on local station WGES. Rev. Leaner was so popular that he was given a separate non-religious slot, complete with advertising, which he filled with swing music. By the Fifties he was the biggest DJ in the city and had progressed to launching R&B record labels.

Al Benson

When we met Al Benson it seemed there was very little that was religious about him. By then approaching 50, he was slick, snappy dressing, jive-talking and a little crude for the tastes of other successful or professional members of the black community. He didn't care: his fans were less sophisticated, generally younger and loved his colourful language. Even more important, there were thousands of them and they would fill seats at the Regal many times over.

Located in Bronzeville – known as the Black Metropolis - on the south side of Chicago, the Regal was a key institution in of one of America's largest concentrations of black business and culture. It's almost pointless listing all the famous African American artists who played the Regal since its opened in 1928. From the stars of the Jazz Age such as Cab Calloway and Duke Ellington, Bronzeville local Nat 'King' Cole, through R&B and Motown, they were all on that stage at some point. Pre-dating Harlem's Apollo by six years, it was more elegant, lavishly decorated and seated twice as many visitors.

Performing here was a huge achievement for anyone; for five white boys from New York, it was an honour.

******

Arriving at the hotel late on the Thursday night, Larry and I roomed together for a change, while Eddie shared with Bobby and Jerry. Irv had arranged a real dive which we had to suffer for the next seven nights, a small, old, shitty hotel on the south side, just a stone's throw from the theater. No wonder I didn't go straight back after the show for the whole week; in fact, I did my best to amuse myself elsewhere and made sure I spent as few hours as possible in that miserable room. On the first night I just couldn't settle, lying in bed repeatedly tapping the old, green metal headboard behind me.

"Neeeiiilll... Stop iiittt!" moaned Larry as he grew increasingly irritated. It eventually became a game: more tapping attracted a complaint with a sillier, more whining sound. Larry tried hard to keep it light and inject some humour into the situation, but for someone who hated every aspect of touring apart from his short time on stage, this was killing him.

We wasted no time heading for the theater the next day, mainly to flee our accommodation, but also because we were excited to see the legendary establishment. We weren't disappointed when we arrived as we saw the impressive columns that supported the different tiers and glimpsed the velvet seats from backstage. As was almost always the case, however, the dressing room was a single, large, shared area in total chaos. On the plus side, numbers were lower than they might have been because there were only two groups on the bill – us and the Dells.

The vibe felt generally more friendly than the Apollo and we seemed more readily accepted as the only white act on the bill. It was all about the music and, in that regard, we were already respected by the other acts for our ability. Titus Turner was in his mid-20s, although he looked younger. His early recording career had not been spectacularly successful, but he had established himself as a very solid songwriter, having penned the Little Willie John hit *All Around the World.* He went on to write for Ray Charles, Dinah Washington and other big names, while continuing to make records with more of a soul direction. They suited his expressive voice, which wouldn't have cut it in a harmony group, but more than did the job. Good guy.

Two musicians in the line-up had played together a lot, but that week each was appearing in his own right. The 40-year-old Frankie Lee Sims was a pioneer of electric blues guitar and cousin of blues legend Lightnin' Hopkins, one of Al Silver's first big signings. He looked like a cleaned-up bluesman from the south: the brim of his hat was pushed high up on his face and his hand was never without a guitar. Frankie was a serious looking dude and was definitely serious about the blues. When we worked alongside him he'd recently made some good records on Ace, the famous R&B label, but none had been smashes. I liked *What Will Lucy Do?*, which had a great driving beat, but Frankie had the singing voice of an old bluesman. Possibly not what most teenagers wanted to buy. One of his collaborators was drummer Jimmy Mullins, who performed as 'Mercy Baby'. Unsurprisingly also on Ace, he played his two singles in Chicago that week: *Marked Deck* and *Silly Dilly Woman*, the first being an exciting and danceable blues number with Frankie's great guitar licks softened by the band's honky tonk piano and breathy sax. I remember feeling that the Mello-Kings' music was very 'clean cut' compared with the dirtier sound of Frankie and Jimmy. I don't know what they made of five very young guys in matching outfits: they didn't show much interest in us and it was both the first and last time we appeared with them.

November 8, 1957 was a big night in rock and roll: it marked the release of Elvis Presley's third movie, *Jailhouse Rock*, a more edgy and exciting offering than *Love me Tender* or *Loving You*. It was eagerly anticipated by his many millions of fans and lines would be forming outside movie theaters. But music fans were already waiting outside the Regal and many would be turned away, to be told to come back on one of the next six nights to see the same acts. In line with previous tours, we started quite early on the bill, but the pleasing reception we were given bumped us up to the position just before the headline act – the Dells.

Originally a high school group like us, the Dells had a three to four years head start. In 1955 they'd scored a million selling #4 hit on the R&B chart with *Oh What A Night*, a slow and steady but beautiful doo-wop song that might have slotted very easily into our own repertoire. In truth, Jerry and Eddie would have struggled to match the accuracy and piercing, clean tones of the Dells' high harmonies, but we'd have still done a decent job. In any case, it's still one of my favourite songs from any era and I was delighted to hear it live in Chicago. The Dells were the real deal among vocal groups and a great bunch of guys too. Later I would spend some quality time with them.

The crowd was well fired up when Benson appeared from the wings, followed by the spotlight, grinning from ear to ear as he strode quickly to the front of the stage. He had put on yet another great show in this important theater, had made a bunch of money and was having a great time. He might have also been a little high.

"We have two very cool groups to end the show now: first the Mello-Kings, from New York, then our closing act the Dells, big stars who need no introduction from me. First I'd like the Mello-Kings to come to the front, and then the Dells, please get into place behind them, ready to sing. Guys, take it away!"

We were onstage at the Regal, with one of the biggest R&B acts in the country standing behind us. Better still, they loved our singing and were grooving in the background as we performed. There could be no better endorsement that we were both cool and talented, a view that the packed house seemed to share when we'd finished. The applause and cheers echoed around the plush auditorium.

Al Benson walked on to the stage as the clapping continued, showing no sign of stopping. It calmed as he attempted to speak for the second time.

"You see, ladies and gentlemen, it goes to prove that you don't have to be black to be talented."

The Dells

A murmur of chuckling, then more applause, though in agreement rather than liking his quip.

Swapping positions with the Dells, we were delighted to be swaying and smiling behind them onstage as they played an amazing set. That arrangement only happened once during that week; it was a spur-of-the-moment idea of Benson's and anyone in the house watching the Mello-Kings and the Dells together that night would have caught something very special.

******

Mabel Smith had been rebranded 'Big Maybelle' by Fred Mendelsohn, the Okeh Records producer who later became the founder and original boss of the Mello-Kings' record label, Herald. It was a snappier stage name, although in truth Mabel wasn't particularly large: slightly bigger than Ella Fitzgerald and a good deal smaller than Big Mama Thornton. Always beautifully dressed in a sophisticated way, Maybelle's round face and smiling eyes were immaculately made up, her ruby red lipstick sealing the confident package. She had released four nor particularly successful singles in in 1957, but the crowd wanted to hear her huge R&B hit from the previous year, *Candy*. In those days, when an artist's older releases didn't hang around for longer on Apple or Spotify or Amazon Music, singing something that wasn't current would have been quite unusual. Maybelle was happy to oblige, gently swinging her wide hips and shaking her head as she got into the groove of her song, from time to time shifting her otherwise silky-smooth voice into a sassy rasp. She was a real class act who should have been a much bigger star on the soul scene years later.

The other solo female singer playing the Regal that week couldn't have been more different. Priscilla Bowman was a slim, glamorous *chanteuse*. Like Maybelle, however, her career was flatlining at that point and the Al Benson gig would have been great exposure to an enthusiastic audience of diehard R&B fans. Priscilla had scored a Number One hit on two years previously with *Hands Off*, a jumpy, upbeat twelve-bar blues that she sang fronting the Jay McShann Orchestra. The song was to bear a strong resemblance to the later blues standard *Got My Mojo Working* by Red Foster. Elvis mashed both together in a medley in the Seventies. Priscilla's slinky dresses and cool demeanour made her rather unapproachable,

Priscilla Bowman with Jay McShann

especially to a bunch of youngsters like us. She looked kind of 'expensive' with her short, straightened and combed forward black hair – looking back, it was a bit 'Mr Spock' - and, at 29, she was no Chantel or Bobbette. The other reason not to get too familiar with Priscilla was that she was Joe Louis's girlfriend.

The former Heavyweight Champion of the World, unbeaten for 14 years until 1950 and, to some, still to this day the greatest heavyweight boxer of all time, was in the house that week. Joe was still married to his second wife (he went on to have two more) but discreetly enjoyed the company of many ladies, some better known than others, along the way. At not even 6’2’’, Louis was shorter than most heavyweights in recent years, with the exception of Mike Tyson, but the guy just exuded power and force – not only to a slender 5’7’’ teenager. His wide back and thick neck simply said ‘stay away’. He was known for rarely cracking a smile, generally only allowing himself one after a win, and backstage at the Regal was no different. The Brown Bomber clearly didn’t want to draw undue attention to himself, which was wishful thinking, while possibly also conscious that he might be pictured with someone other than Mrs. Louis on his arm. It would have taken a brave photographer.

The Mello-Kings were all standing near the wings, nudging each other and gesturing towards Louis. I kept thinking how thrilled my Dad would have been: he was a huge boxing fan and had followed Louis closely over the years. I still think he’d have been too awestruck to approach him. It would have been extremely uncool for me to wander over and say hi while Louis was watching Priscilla do her magic out there. After several minutes of staring, I managed to catch the big guy’s eye momentarily when he turned round. I nodded respectfully, acknowledging I’d recognised him and showing my pleasure at seeing him there. He nodded back, stony faced as usual, but returning sufficient respect for someone who was performing alongside his girlfriend. They were a golden few seconds.

******

I would have felt far less cool if the sports hero had been backstage to witness one of the most embarrassing foul-ups of our career, which also happened in Regal week. As had been the case in Buffalo, it wasn't our fault; in fact, we were victims of our own successful set on the third night in Chicago, when we had left the crowd begging for more. After returning to the stage to take a second bow, blowing kisses with a kick of the foot towards the audience, we retreated to find that they still hadn't settled. Benson offered us the opportunity to sing an encore; trouble was, we hadn't rehearsed anything suitable for such an occurrence. After some quick deliberation amongst ourselves, we told the band we'd go for *Honey Honey*, a song Jerry liked that we all knew pretty well. It had been a minor hit that year for Frankie Lymon's kid brother, Lewis, with his group the Teenchords. We clearly knew it better than the band. Leaving us shuffling around for too long while they agreed the right key, or whatever, the drummer finally hit the skins - with the intro to another song. The uptempo first bars of *Honey Honey* had been replaced by a rather slower 'kick-snare-kick-kick-snare' from the beginning of *Money Honey*, an early hit for the Drifters. Astonishingly, Jerry continued singing his song while the band carried on with theirs. Meanwhile Eddie and I were making light of the situation, doing our dance routine to the terrible combined tunes, me doing the splits and Eddie 'pushing' my head up and down three times, complete with pointing to the audience before the last one. I glimpsed Levister in the wings, hands over his ears; in his gravelly voice, he kept shouting, "Oh no! My God!!!" The audience was in hysterics, but laughing with, not at, us. They could see we were pros and, after all, had asked for this encore. Again, it ended amid the most incredible applause, but we'd had our second bite of the cherry and had to make way for the next act.

There must have been something weird about that drummer, because the Dells' Chuck Barksdale had big problems with him too.

On the first night they had walked on to play *Oh What A Night*, the man with the sticks was missing his cue and coming in late with the wrong beat. Very unamused, Chuck had to haul him back into time by signalling repeatedly with his finger until they were all together.

"I'm going to have to show him how to do it," Chuck said afterwards, shaking his head. He was rattled and didn't want it to happen again. I'm not sure if a percussion lesson ever took place between the two, but the next night the issue had been fixed – just – with the house band's drummer watching Chuck's finger carefully throughout the performance of their biggest hit.

Anyway, our own fiasco had been long forgotten by the time the show ended and everyone was back in the dressing room. Nobody mentioned it and definitely not Al Benson, who was in his own closed dressing room, smoking pot with Maybelle. The pungent vapor was escaping under the door and into the corridor. It all seemed very exotic to us: we were abundantly aware of drugs, soft and hard – our heavy schedule on the road had educated us in that respect – but that side of the rock and roll life was of no interest to us. Personally, I just wanted to hang out with the Dells.

******

As Illinois natives, growing up in Harvey, just 30 minutes outside Chicago, the Dells knew their way around the city very well. By 'the city', I mean the black south side, with all its vibrant nightlife, entertainment and amusements. The group had originally been six: Marvin Junior, Verne Allison, Johnny Funches, drum critic Chuck and brothers Michael and Lucius McGill, but Lucius quit ahead of their first record deal. Johnny had written *Oh What A Night*, on which he sang co-lead with Marvin. I formed a good friendship with the guys that week, seemingly without any other Mello-Kings. We

Big Maybelle, 1957

had all got on very well together in and around the Regal, but I guess I was a little less reserved than the others (perhaps excluding Eddie) and always found it easy to strike up a conversation with people (perhaps excluding Joe Louis). The Dells' style had impressed me: they wore well cut suits, sometimes tuxedos and other times dark two-pieces with silk pocket handkerchiefs, but in a week at the Regal were never seen in the same outfits twice, at least not two nights running. Oh, and the time they would spend on their hair! Michael's was an impressively pomaded pile, almost a pompadour, with a parting on one side that might have been made with a small axe. It was a sight to behold. He kept it in place ahead of going on stage by using a red satin 'wrap' to stop the pomade melting into his eyes, while preventing the weight of the bouffant thatch flopping forward.

It was Michael, Johnny and I who became good buddies in Chicago from the first night. I really related to them and respected their professionalism, their work ethic and the way they handled themselves: no smoking, drinking or messing about; just making great music. They treated me like a brother as they showed me around, often the only white face to be seen in the nightspots we visited. One highlight was a very old fashioned, run down pool hall where we spent many hours playing while, in the background, a small and elderly black gentleman in a white jacket seemed totally out of place shining patrons' shoes as they sat in a high chair. My greatest memory, however, was our trip to see the famous Four Step Brothers in their dance show at Chicago's most glamorous nightclub, Chez Paree, in the north of the city. The guys use their local celebrity to sneak me in - nothing to do with being white; I was clearly underage by some way.

******

At the end of the week, after parting with a healthy slice of our earnings for our agent, we shared $860 between five of us – almost $9,000 as I write this – although we didn't get paid until our return to New York. It wasn't a bad deal for having a lot of fun and, in my case, among the greatest days of my career. In our own small way, we had conquered Chicago, the Mecca of the genuine R&B star: no small feat for five mainly teenage white guys in 1957. The experience would be hard to beat.

Chapter 9

City of Oaks

UNTIL I visited Raleigh, North Carolina at the age of seventeen, I guess I had never encountered 'normalised' racial segregation in everyday life, or at least its strict enforcement. New York City and its suburbs were possibly as relaxed towards race as you would ever find in those days, even within the generally liberal northern states. Mount Vernon was a cultural melting pot and everyone rubbed along pretty well. It was by no means perfect harmony, or without tension, but I can only speak from my own experience: I had several black friends – as well as buddies from other ethnic backgrounds - through school, sport and music; the circles I mixed in were not only inclusive, but would not have tolerated casual racism. In terms of our 'art', the Mello-Kings clearly owed its vocal approach to the blues and gospel traditions of black music. As you've already gathered, we actually aspired to perform in historically black venues and to black audiences.

Everyone knows that 'The South' in 1957 was very different. Raleigh and its surroundings had very 'live' issues about race at the time we visited. Nearby Durham was the location of the famous Royal Ice Cream sit-in, in June 1957, when a group of African

American protesters entered the Royal Ice Cream Parlor and sat in the section reserved for white customers. While the protesters failed to appeal their trespass convictions, the unplanned event influenced civil rights strategies in the years that immediately followed. It's safe to say that summer was not the time for us to sail into town and test the racial boundaries.

Raleigh was a hell of a long way to go for a one nighter – more than 10 hours from home in the car – but Al Silver said it was a great opportunity to promote *Tonite, Tonite* in a region way further south than our natural Tri-State touring area and a chance to appear on local TV in North Carolina. We'd be casting our net wider. White rock and roll was really taking off in the south east, boosted by the established country scene spawning new talent, and southern teenagers were buying more 45s. Ironically, over that period the state produced some of the most successful black musical artists of all time: Roberta Flack, Nina Simone, Ben E King, Wilbert Harrison, Clyde McPhatter of the Drifters, and our fellow doo-woppers, the 5 Royales. The guys and I had been given our instructions in the Herald offices and were getting in the elevator on our way out when we realized we'd forgotten the expense check of $500.

"Neil, will you go back and get it while we wait here?" said Bobby.

Nobody else liked dealing with the money at that time – although it barely hit their pockets before it was spent – and more often than not it fell to me to talk to Al Silver. I knocked on the door of his office, where he appeared to be in deep conversation with his accountant.

"I tell you, this is going to be my biggest hit ever," he was saying to the guy, before spying me hovering in the doorway.

Al Silver, 1957

"What do you want?" he yelled at me, clearly unhappy to have been overheard. Arrangements for the timing and size of payments from Herald to the Mello-Kings were opaque, to say the least and, apart from monies from performances which were mostly arranged by Irv Nahan, revenues from record sales seemed to be quickly absorbed by studio expenses, marketing and travel. True, our biggest hits hadn't been written by us, so that slice of the pie was never going to come our way, but one way or another, like so many other groups at the time, we never made much from that side of the business. In any event, Al didn't like talking money with us.

"We don't have the expenses check," I said.

Al glared at me before turning to the accountant. "Give him the check,' he snarled. The note in question was torn out of its book and handed to me.

"Now get out!" Al yelled again.

******

Another Al had been charged to drive us all the way to Raleigh. Long-time Herald artist Al Savage was a trusted associate of Al Silver. A consistently, but only moderately successful solo singer of cheerful, unremarkable R&B songs, Savage released 11 singles on Herald between 1953 and 1957, often touring alongside Faye Adams or the Turbans to promote the records. His tenth release, *Happy Tears*, was recorded not long before we were signed to the label. Leaving New York at early breakfast time, seven of us (Levister came too) managed to squeeze into Savage's Cadillac, three upfront and four behind, and we set off on our strange road trip to Raleigh, the 'City of Oaks'. Cruising on the newly opened I-95, we crossed New Jersey, Philadelphia, Maryland, DC and the east side of Virginia before passing into North Carolina.

HERALD's HOT in '57

Both sides breaking

Al Savage

"HAPPY TEARS"

"STILL IN LOVE WITH YOU"

H - 494

Richmond, Norfolk, Durham, New Orleans, Chicago

The Nutmegs

"COMIN' HOME"

H - 492

Butchie Saunders

"GREAT BIG HEART"

H - 491

Richmond, Norfolk, Hartford

The Turbans

"VALLEY OF LOVE"

H - 495

It was a mind-numbingly boring journey but Al, a friendly, large black guy in his late 20s with big hair, was good company and we all made the best of being thrown together for 48 hours. It was almost certainly not what Al had in mind when he bought his fancy Cadillac.

We had stopped a couple of times along the way and made good time earlier in the drive, so, knowing that we were unlikely to get a chance to eat before the show later, we pulled into a diner not long after crossing the border into North Carolina sometime mid-afternoon. Levister had told us of his sister's warning that he should never cross the Mason-Dixon line, and he was about to prove her right for the first, but not last time in those two days. Entering the diner I saw something I'd only ever heard about at school, but never thought I'd witness in person: segregated eating areas for blacks and whites. We all looked at each other with blank expressions of embarrassment before Savage and Levister headed one way and the Mello-Kings the other.

Our waitress lightened the mood on our table. A cute little blonde with an endearing southern drawl, we obviously had to ask her name.

"Georgia," she responded with a smile.

Our response might have been predictable, but was well received. One by one, we broke into our respective harmonies to deliver a well-practised rendition of Hoagy Carmichael's song. It would be another three years before Ray Charles recorded it.

The girl blushed at the unexpected tribute and skipped off smiling to place our orders after indulging us for a minute. We, however, were just getting into our stride. It's amazing that our spirits were so high after being crammed into a car on a hot day for ten hours, but very little would ever stop us singing. The harmonies were soaring and the volume was creeping up steadily - to a point where whatever frequency we were generating began to make the air conditioning grille rattle. The diner wasn't packed and there were certainly no complaints, but as we left I felt a bit weird that the Mello-Kings had been having fun in the white section while our co-passengers (an odd one-off pairing with nothing in common but the color of their skin) had to eat elsewhere.

But this was only the beginning. Within an hour of setting off again, we arrived at the appointed meeting place in Raleigh from which we would be taken on to the TV studio by one of the station's representatives. We were greeted on the steps of the Wake County courthouse, possibly not the friendliest choice of landmark, by an attractive and formidable looking lady in her 30s. She was dressed very fine in an unmistakeably southern style: white dress, white hat and matching shoes; the ensemble was teamed with a suitably superior expression on her perfectly made-up face. Glued to the steps, she beckoned us over with a lazy hand gesture, her immaculately organised paperwork nestling under her other arm.

"Are you the Mello-Kings?"

"Yes, we are."

Then, while avoiding looking directly at Savage and Levister, the woman said coolly:

"The two niggers stay, or I leave and you don't go anywhere."

Shocked, I broke involuntarily into a nervous laugh. I was quite in awe of the woman's boldness. She was absolutely serious about this dealbreaker. Eddie didn't help by beginning to snicker uncontrollably, presumably also a result of embarrassment, but it wasn't helpful. Our black colleagues stood calmly in the background, fully conscious of what was going on, before walking to the Cadillac with all the dignity they could muster and high-tailing it away from the scene. The woman directed the five of us to another large car and we were driven off in silence to our TV session on the other side of town.

Wake County Courthouse

******

Teenage dance shows were beginning to spring up on TV all over the country. The revamped *American Bandstand* under Dick Clark was about to launch, but had been beaten to the air by *The Milt Grant Show*, a popular Washington DC based program on WTTG whose audience remained undented by its new Philly rival. They were both followed by *The Buddy Deane Show* in Baltimore and, a little later, *Seventeen* from WOI-TV near Des Moines, Iowa. In parallel *The Mitch Thomas Show* showcased black talent to a black audience from Wilmington, Delaware. Interestingly, the year after we visited Raleigh, new TV station WRAL recruited black DJ J.D. Lewis from its radio arm to host a groundbreaking, inclusive new dance show, *Teenage Frolics*.

Arriving with our scary escort at the TV station, one again we wondered why we had travelled so far to make this appearance. The studio was far from glamorous, with a small-town vibe. We were allowed a tiny office to use as dressing room and, after getting changed, we were led by a pleasant young woman towards where the action seemed to be. This was not a dance show, or even a music program, but a talk show that featured musical special guests. The presenter, a very well turned out, handsome young dude, was genuinely pleased to see us.

"Guys, thanks so much for making the trip all the way down here to see us. It's really great having you on the show," he enthused. We couldn't have been made more welcome, despite the inauspicious start to our short time in Raleigh.

When our segment of the show arrived, after a brief introduction we grinned and swayed through the jaunty introduction to *Do Baby Do* before lip synching expertly to our harmonies. The reception from the studio audience was lively, within the bounds of a show that wasn't normally geared to featuring teen idols, and the smiling presenter came over to our spot on the open floor to make small talk. He ran through our names, introducing us to the viewers one by one with a camera close-up, and namechecked Mount Vernon. Standard, meaningless TV stuff, really.

"Now the guys are going to sing us their new record, which is already gaining momentum in the chart. This time with *Tonite, Tonite*, it's the Mello-Kings!"

Some medium-strength applause, which the studio manager allowed to die down before starting the tape, and then Bobby joined in perfectly with the vocal intro. It was a very simple gig and it eased us into the punishing schedule of touring that was to follow. Al Silver had also been right about Raleigh being useful for marketing: as the record began its long chart run in August, a cover version was unhelpfully also released on another label, the Nashville based Athens Records. Country singer Andy Wilson had recorded a very attractive, to be fair, crooning version of our hit,

ANDY WILSON
(Athens 700)

B "LITTLE MAMA" [Cedarwood BMI—Worthan, Walker] The Athens label bows on the disk scene with an excellent first release featuring Andy Wilson. Commercial rock-a-billy side with a good lyric and equally solid beat. Side has potential and deserves attention.

B "TONITE TONITE" [Angel BMI —Myles] A pretty fish beat ballad is chanted with style and tenderness by the mellow voiced crooner. Lovely teenage fare that becomes prettier with each listen. Kids'll go for both halves.

complete with lush orchestration. It was the B-side to *Little Mama*, a rockabilly number more in line with his usual output. Cash Box reviewed it favourably: "A pretty fish beat ballad is chanted with style and tenderness. Lovely teenage fare that becomes prettier with each listen. Kids'll go for both halves."

Anyway, we'd done as we were told and, apart from more than 20 hours' driving, a night in shitty (separate) hotels and two racist incidents endured by our colleagues in one afternoon, it had been relatively painless. Al Savage had been paid by Herald to chauffeur us, but I felt sorry for Levister, who had completely wasted his time and been insulted, into the bargain. Raleigh was the farthest south we ever played and we never returned. In fact, we couldn't get out of there fast enough the next morning.

Chapter 10

Monkey business in DC

THE Mello-Kings' punishing schedule was turned up a few notches in the second half of September 1957 when Irv booked us for back-to-back weeks in Washington DC and Baltimore. Again, it was part of a package with what seemed like a really random mix of artists, some of them pretty big. Apart from being just plain exhausting, it was one of the wildest, most raucous and certainly worst organised times we had as performers.

Still driven around by Chico at that time, the five of us plus Levister crammed into the car and headed first for the capital. In hindsight, I'm not sure why Levister came at all; he wasn't paid for being there and surely he could have been gainfully employed playing piano somewhere back home in those two weeks. Perhaps he felt a sense of 'ownership' towards part of our set, having written *Do Baby Do*, although he was rarely, if ever, involved in the arrangement that was played by whichever backing band we were given on the night. The drive was a little over four hours, so not too painful. The memory of the journey that really stuck with me was constantly thinking "Yikes! I have another two weeks off school." I may have been having the time of my life, but I still cared about my school career – possibly more than the others did about theirs. When I first went to A.B. Davis it was with the intention of eventually getting to college to play basketball. I wanted to make something of myself; if it wasn't in music, then it would need to be something else. Being a deadbeat wasn't an option.

There were no hotels involved this time: Irv had arranged a house for us to stay in over the two week period; Chico drove us back and forth to Baltimore on the second leg of that tour, an hour's journey using a new section of road that had opened only weeks before. We were impressed when we arrived at the DC house, a large residence with a bedroom each that was typically rented to musical artists for several days or even weeks at a time. The owner must have made a fortune because, as far as we could make out, it was never empty and had been inhabited by some great names of rock and roll in the mid-1950s. There was a lot of space and we could eat there, keep all our wardrobe items safe and hang out in comfort. Best of all, it was no more than five minutes from the famous Howard Theater, which was where we were playing. Less than two miles north of Capitol Hill, it was also very close to the now razed Griffith Stadium, home of both the Senators major league baseball team and the Redskins NFL team. We were able to hear the stadium crowd roar a number of times during our two week residency but sadly didn't get a chance to catch a game.

At 17, this was the largest city I'd been to outside of New York in my near-adult life. I had actually visited DC once or twice before when I was younger, since my mom's brother, Uncle Bart Albero – my favourite uncle - was stationed at Bolling Air Base in the early Fifties. I enjoyed being back in my own right, doing important, grown up things in an important place. The Howard Theater only reinforced how cool it was to be working in the capital. Predating both the Apollo and the Regal, the grand entrance to the Howard had welcomed well-to-do black audiences since before World War

One. Now slightly faded, but still imposing, the theater's middle-aged classical and jazz concertgoers had made way for a much younger audience eager to see the latest R&B acts. They weren't going to be disappointed. Topping the bill that week was the great Larry Williams, supported by Huey 'Piano' Smith and his Clowns, a rare mixed black and white doo-wop act, the Del Vikings, and our old friend Screamin' Jay Hawkins.

******

The Del-Vikings had many personnel changes in the Fifties. At one stage there were two connected groups of the same name. Originally formed in 1955 by a bunch of Pennsylvania based US Air Force guys, led by Clarence Quick and original lead singer Kripp Johnson, when we met them two years later they had been joined by two white singers: baritone David Lerchey and tenor Gus Backus. The hit version of the group's best known song, *Come Go with Me*, was sung by Gus. It was a million-seller and later featured in several movies set in the Fifties and Sixties. We seemed to get on fine with the guys, although they seemed kind of a strange collection: more life experience than us at a relatively young age, including in the service, but surprisingly immature in other ways, as we'd later find in Baltimore. They definitely thought they were a lot funnier than others found them.

Huey Smith and his Clowns, however, were a genuine hoot. We worked alongside their classic line up at the time that their first huge hit, *Rocking Pneumonia and the Boogie Woogie Flu* was released. The core trio was led by Huey, a slim, sharp suited and permanently smiling black guy from New Orleans who had cut his musical teeth on the southern R&B of Professor Longhair before starting his rock and roll career playing piano in Little Richard's band. In the year we played Washington together, Huey had joined forces with Bobby Marchan, a flamboyant singer in his late 20s who had operated for some years as a female impersonator. While the million selling, gold disc awarded *Rocking Pneumonia* featured a longer cast of male singers in the studio, the touring Clowns in late summer 1957 were completed by a hilarious young lady, Gerri Hall. It was impossible not to like Gerri, who had either been nicknamed or renamed herself after crazy comedian Jerry Lewis because of her similar onstage antics. Like Huey and Bobby, she was a proper singer and musician, but strongly believed that having fun while working was the most important thing. Formerly married to Fats Domino's brother-in-law, Gerri met her fellow Clowns when waiting tables at the Dew Drop Inn, the famous New Orleans R&B joint. I enjoyed keeping track of her career over the years, which included a spell as one of Ray Charles's Raelettes.

Rocking Pneumonia remains a great song that I always turn up louder if it comes on the radio, which isn't often enough. It was written as a light hearted reference to a huge Asian flu bug that was sweeping America at that time. Some say it rhymed with a specific condition called 'walking pneumonia'. It never came up in conversation with Huey, so I have no idea if it's true, but imagine in 2022 writing a million-selling hit song about the coronavirus!

******

It was undoubtedly Larry Williams who made the greatest impression on the Mello-Kings during that tour. Larry was in the early stages of becoming a major star and a very influential songwriter. He was an important part of rock and roll history and his role is possibly underplayed, although he inspired some great names over the years. The Beatles, in particular John Lennon, were

Huey Smith and his Clowns

huge fans and recorded several of his songs throughout the band's life and individually beyond. Even so, it wasn't Larry's material that left his mark on us: he was very, very cool; and he was wild.

The New Orleans R&B scene that migrated performers into the north east states in the mid-to-late Fifties included many connected artists. Most of those acts knew each other, shared musicians and became good friends. They also set the bar high for us New Yorkers putting our own twist on black music. Larry was part of that gang: in his late teens he would help his cousin, New Orleans singer Lloyd Price, driving him to gigs and using the opportunity to learn a performer's stagecraft; Huey Smith played with Price, and obviously also with Little Richard, who was Larry's label-mate at Speciality Records. When Richard temporarily left rock for religion in 1957, Specialty was keen for Larry to step into his shoes. Over the two years that followed, Larry scored many hits – *Bony Moronie, Dizzy Miss Lizzie, Slow Down, She Said Yeah*, to name just a few – but it was his second success, *Short Fat Fannie*, that was riding high when we met him.

Hot on the heels of *High School Dance*, which was released again as a B-side, *Short Fat Fannie* was a million seller for Larry and the song that every kid wanted to hear in the Howard that week. *Fannie* was one of rock and roll's first 'novelty' songs – think *Splish Splash* or, later, *Rubber Ball* – and told a story that namechecked other songs of the day: *Long Tall Sally*, *Rip It Up*, *Heartbreak Hotel*, *Blue Suede Shoes*, *Blueberry Hill* and many more. It was a great crowd pleaser and sung in an exciting, shouty style that owed a lot to Little Richard. When I play those records now I remember that I hadn't thought much of Larry's voice at the time; then again, he wasn't from the world of modern harmony like us, and his singing got the job done more than adequately.

It was Larry's bold move to trump Little Richard's outrageousness that really got the DC audiences going – except it wasn't just him doing the screaming and hollering. For reasons I still can't work out, the bill-topper decided to bring a monkey on stage with him. I can only imagine it was meant to be an amusing gimmick and, at least when they were both front-of-house, it was very popular. Larry would emerge from the wings, handsome and ice-cool in a beautifully cut suit, walking the monkey who was wearing a collar attached to a chain. The also cool and relaxed demeanor of the monkey added to the hilarity, but that was just the start of it. As the band started and Larry sat at the piano, he would proceed to sing *Short Fat Fannie* to the ape. The crowd cried helplessly with laughter as the wrinkled face with its sparkly eyes looked up adoringly at Larry, who sang the kooky love song with all the comic sincerity he could gather. Occasionally the animal whooped with delight. It was a hell of a spectacle. I can't remember if the 'primate stagemate' was a boy or a girl, but I don't suppose it mattered.

The stunt ended the show on a fun note and, in terms of craziness, outdid both Little Richard and the tour's resident lunatic, Jay Hawkins. The only problem arose when the monkey wasn't on stage. What do you do with a creature like that for the other 23 hours and 45 minutes every day for a week? Larry had to keep the monkey in a cage somewhere at the back of the theater. This really amused Eddie, who took great delight in taunting it every time he walked past.

"Hey! Short Fat Fannie!" Eddie would tease over and over again. It probably wasn't only Eddie's fault, but after a while the monkey, deciding it was bored with its incarceration and the lack of affection shown by passing R&B artists, retaliated by throwing its own shit out of the cage. Unsurprisingly, the Howard's janitors were furious. Having already seen the class of performer in the theatre plummet from opera singers to jazzers to teen idols in a short few years, they were now cleaning up monkey turds. Quite rightly, Larry had to pay the guys extra to keep them sweet until we moved on to Baltimore.

****

Eddie's monkey business backstage showed how we struggled to amuse ourselves in the considerable downtime we had while in DC. The late Charlie Watts of the Rolling Stones famously described his first 25 years in the band as five years of playing and 20 years of hanging around. The Mello-Kings did a lot of that on tour. Promoters and stage managers wanted artists on site so that they could keep control of the show. I suppose it made sense if they were effectively working with a bunch of kids and sometimes some overgrown ones like Jay Hawkins and Larry Williams. Sure, there were rehearsals and sound checks every day, but they didn't really take up much time. One afternoon, Chico suggested he and Eddie and I should take a drive around to explore the city. It was a great idea until we got badly lost and had to resort to asking for help from people on the sidewalk, all of whom sent us in conflicting directions. I'd like to think this wasn't deliberate. In the end we were extremely lucky to make it back to the Howard in time for that evening's show.

There were consolations. As the week progressed and reviews of our performances became increasingly positive, the number of chicks waiting for us at the stage door at the end of the show grew night after night. But the teenage adulation was worth nothing compared to the satisfaction of being congratulated by a real star who'd enjoyed our set. That was the case when we met the great Bo Diddley after an early show. Still in his clean-cut phase in those days, yet already becoming eccentric in his dress and showy personality, Bo had actually taken the time to seek us out at the Howard's stage door. Lucky for me and Eddie, he found us; the other three, as usual, had skedaddled as soon as we'd gotten changed. Bo echoed every other traditional R&B musician who came into contact with us.

"I just had to come by and see you guys because I really thought you were black! That was a great set, I loved it."

We laughed and talked for a while with Bo about the music we liked, where else we had toured, that kind of thing.

"I'm gonna get something to eat – come on, I'll treat you," said Bo. We followed the heavy set young star out of stage door. He walked between me and Eddie as we took a right and headed down the street to his favourite café – he was living nearby at the time -

Larry Williams 1957

passers-by recognising the distinctive black hat with its white band, which on that day was teamed with a black vest and matching pants. Hanging with Bo Diddley remains one of my coolest memories; praise about our act from a giant like him in 1957, the heyday of rock and roll, stayed with me forever.

******

Back at our rented house, the strains of the five of being locked up together for a week were beginning to weigh heavily on the Mello-Kings. I had spent most of my time in DC with Eddie or, at the Howard, hanging out with the other artists. While the house was in a central location, the neighborhood wasn't great and we weren't tempted to go out and look around. Remember, we were still too young to go to bars and clubs, even if they hadn't been sleezy dives. It's no surprise that we spent the rest of the evening doing what any other group of five immature, overconfident young guys away from home and bored out of their minds would do: we trashed the place. In an innocent, unintentional way, of course, and only as a result of good humored high jinks. As we raced around the house, armed with makeshift pea shooters and hastily gathered buckets of water, the mother of all play fights resulted in total carnage. If Levister had been present, I'd have remembered him having a hilarious meltdown, so I can only assume he'd been out of the house at the time. Either way, there was a good deal of damage, not least the near flooding we had caused. I have no doubt we would have been fined by the landlord for this; presumably it would have been added to the long list of additional costs on our account that seemed to shrink our pop star earnings.

Bo Diddley and the Twang Machine guitar built for him by Gretsch

Chapter 11

Good Morning Baltimore

OUR nice house (before we trashed it) in a less nice neighborhood of central DC turned out to be a sanctuary when we returned every night from Baltimore. The tedious commute in the second week of a that tour was a blessing in disguise: we couldn't wait to get out of town as soon as the show was over.

The first night at Baltimore's Royal Theater was Friday 27 September 1957. Another 'Chitlin Circuit' establishment, the Royal had presented all the big names of jazz and blues to a 95% black audience since 1922: Cab Calloway, Pearl Bailey, Duke Ellington, Louis Armstrong, Nat King Cole – name anyone. Its location, however, was in an area of rapid urban decay. The streets around that part of Pennsylvania Avenue in West Baltimore City had seen an exodus of middle class residents, both white and black, since the beginning of the Fifties and Old West Baltimore was going downhill fast. Within 15 years of our playing there, the Royal was demolished and pretty much the whole Pennsylvania Avenue corridor went on to be razed. Anyway, you get the picture: it was rough, tough and every night Chico had to park the car as close to the Royal's stage door as possible so that we could get the hell out of Dodge.

Baltimore week was kind of miserable for lots of reasons, some big, some small. Having let off steam in the house and enjoyed the temporary release, we were now living in a mess. Needless to say, none of us was in a rush to tidy the place and Levister's grumpiness was swinging between unintentionally comical outbursts of frustration and passive-aggressive sulking. Then, inevitably, the Asian flu epidemic reached the Mello-Kings. It hit Jerry first and worst, although we all seemed to have it to some degree and were forced to see a doctor to avoid cancelling our set. Jerry missed at least one performance and we had to juggle his parts with Bobby throughout the week.

We had anticipated the flu issue when we were still playing DC. It was already getting out of hand: every act except Jay Hawkins seemed to have been affected in some way, even if it had just been one of their accompanists or backing singers; Huey and Gerri had both been suffering. After discussing it among the Mello-Kings on the last day of the DC leg, it was decided that I should speak to Larry Williams, in his capacity as the headline act, to see if cancelling Baltimore might be the sensible thing to do. I went to see Larry in his dressing room, where he was applying his pomade carefully; his straightened hair already looked as if it had been parted with the Dells' ax.

"Hey Larry, me and the Mello-Kings were just thinking about next week's shows. Almost everyone's sick. The whole thing seems to be crapping out. Don't you think we should call the promoter and cancel Baltimore?"

Larry set down the jar of green gunk and turned to face me from his seat. He fixed me with his narrowed eyes, trying to assess if the young guy he had chatted with all week was turning out to be an idiot.

"Come on, man! We can't do that! The show must go on. We can't give up this bread!" Larry knew that cancelling would mean refunding tickets, an angry promoter who'd be reluctant to work with him again and, ultimately, no pay. We never spoke about it again. Everyone had flu shots in Baltimore, but there was no way I was going to agree to being injected away from home by a doctor I didn't know.

As if flu wasn't bad enough, Bobby was then hit by what was called 'trench mouth' at the time. We joked that that this nasty oral condition with a World War One nickname was a direct result of too much kissing, but in reality the poor guy had fallen victim to a non-contagious gum disease with terrible inflammation, searing pain and profuse bleeding. It had come out of nowhere. The doctor gave him a bottle of blue stuff to rinse around his mouth and his gappy grin had to remain tinted until the infection had gone. Kissing was the last thing on Bobby's mind.

******

The Royal shows were tense affairs. The aggressive behaviour of youth audiences around the US in earlier years had labelled kids 'juvenile delinquents'. That was when white rock and roll was taking off and the new concept of a teenager, with his or her own musical interests and freedoms, was widely misunderstood by the older generation. But the situation at the Royal was different: a rough crowd out there in the 1,500 seat auditorium, largely made up of young people growing up amid social unrest, and possibly starting to discover drugs, all made for an unforgiving clientele. If there was any delay or hitch whatsoever, they would get restless and irritated; when someone in the crowd shouted out an insult directed towards performers on the stage, the audience would react and escalate the issue. They even threw bottles at the acts, regardless, it seemed, of whether they thought the singers were bad

Baltimore's Royal Theater, 1950s

or good. We had encountered notoriously tough crowds at the Apollo, but the Regal's concertgoers were in another league. Given the high quality bill they were being treated to, with some very big stars, there was no respect whatsoever for the performers.

Larry Williams seemed to take it all in his stride. He was a little older, had seen much more of life than us and was unfazed by thuggish behavior. We never saw the side of Larry Williams that before too long had him tagged as 'the bad boy of rock and roll', but he was rumoured to have links to the criminal underworld. No wonder he didn't care about a few kids with bottles. No stranger to violence and drug abuse, Larry was believed to have operated as a pimp before his musical career. By the end of the Fifties he was getting arrested for possession of narcotics, most likely for supply. The early Sixties saw him in prison for a brief spell. Smooth, cool performer or not, no young delinquent in the Royal's audience was going to fuck with Larry Williams.

Frankly, backstage at the Royal was just as bad that week. There was more messing about among the acts themselves - the tone had definitely been lowered by the shit-slinging monkey in DC – but one of them really crossed the line when we were in our dressing room. Having the Scholl brothers incapacitated in various ways and the rest of us feeling below-par with mild flu, the mood among the Mello-Kings was fractious, to say the least. What happened next was extremely unhelpful.

There was a knock on the dressing room door – surprising in itself, since people generally either burst in or stayed away. I strode to the door, yanked it open and was met by an assault of stinging liquid in my face, accompanied by hysterical laughter from my attackers. It was the Del-Vikings, who had resorted to stupid pranks to keep themselves amused. I couldn't tell exactly which one was the sprayer, but I'm pretty sure it was neither David nor Gus.

"What the fuck are you doing, man?" I howled in pain. They kept laughing, though now more nervously as they realized the full effect of the joke. "Jeez, I think I'm going blind!" My eyes were streaming and I could barely see through their smarting red rims. A small crowd had assembled and we were soon joined by Jay Hawkins. After surveying the situation he hurried away, only to return moments later with a small suitcase.

"Get outta here!" the wild man shouted as he dispersed the onlookers and chased away the Del-Vikings. Jay decided to walk me into his own dressing room to 'treat' my injury. Kneeling down to open the case, he revealed what could only be described as a small pharmacy. No wonder he'd been immune to the flu. In a way I was relieved my poor eyes couldn't see everything in the case, suspecting it wasn't necessarily all for medicinal purposes. The offending blue liquid used by my assailant turned out to be Aqua Velva aftershave. A couple of years earlier, a Norman Rockwell poster had advertised the product as "A Luxury That Actually Does You Good". Those meaningless words couldn't have been further from the truth. They rang loudly in my head as Jay made me lean back and pulled my eyelids apart before rinsing carefully with Murine eye drops. How on earth did he even have those with him? Amazing.

Later that evening a guilty and contrite Del-Viking knocked again on our door.

"Neil, I'm so sorry man, I didn't think it was going to go in your eyes," said the dude as he stood uneasily in the doorway. What the hell did he think was going to happen if he aimed aftershave at my face? He knew it could have been worse; we were both lucky that I hadn't been out of action after that and grateful that Screamin' Dr Jay had been on hand. The episode was soon forgotten and everything was cool with the Del-Vikings after that.

The Del-Vikings, 1957

******

Back at the house in DC there was a letter for me. In fact there was one almost every day – from Mary Ann. I had given her our temporary address and she kept my spirits up, especially in that second week, with amusing trivia about events at school and at home. Mary Ann would write 143 on the back of the envelope where she'd stuck it down. It took me a few days – and an explanation from one of the older guys – before I realized it stood for 'I Love You'. Duh!

Someone else had been trying to get hold of us. Without the benefit of cell phones in those days, Irv had tried to reach us through the theater, to pass on a message from Al Silver who had in turn been contacted by Bob Crewe. It was while on tour in DC and Baltimore that we missed out on Crewe's song *Silhouettes.* As I mentioned before, he gave it to The Rays because we weren't physically available to record it in late September 1957. It was released within three weeks and became a smash hit.

Screamin' Jay Hawkins, 1957

Chapter 12

Frankie, Bobby and George

YOUNGSTOWN, Ohio felt like a strange place for east coast pop artists to tour. Unlike Chicago, where we had already played, it had no meaningful part in the history of R&B, yet it was still a good hike west from our usual circuit. I had no knowledge of Ohio, except that it was the birth-state of one of my biggest musical heroes, Dean Martin, and that Alan Freed came from Columbus. As it turned out, my Aunt Connie actually lived in Youngstown, as did my cousin Basil.

Irv Nahan had booked us back-to-back shows in one night. As was often the case, we had no idea who else was on the bill. He didn't tell us and we didn't ask. Frankly, we were having so much fun we really didn't care too much. So it was a great surprise to find that the list, while short, was very high quality and we were lucky to be included alongside Frankie Avalon, George Hamilton IV and Bobby Darin in the All Star Record Hop at a relatively small venue, the Elms Ballroom.

We met, as we so often did, at Mom's Diner opposite the Lincoln Lounge, then collected the Mello-Bomb from its parking spot at Dick Levister's house on the south side of town. After our Chicago tire episode we were all wondering whether our piece-of-shit car would make it to Ohio, but I got behind the wheel and drove the five of us from Mount Vernon, a distance of more than 400 miles and a journey time of seven hours. We left home mid-morning and were in Youngstown comfortably in time to prepare for the first show at around 6pm. All acts stayed at the same hotel, which had been organised by Irv, but we didn't see anyone else until we got to the theater and couldn't really hang out with the other performers until after the second show. There was no question of Connie – who wasn't actually my aunt, but my mother's younger cousin – having us all to stay in the same way that we were hosted in Philly. All the same, she would have loved to come to the concert and was desperate for a ticket, but I simply couldn't get her in.

Built in the Twenties, the Elms had become a major music venue during the Big Band era. It was located at 529 Elm St. on what is now the campus of Youngstown State University. R&B and rock and roll had continued to supply top live acts in the Fifties and early Sixties: Chuck Berry and Ray Charles both played not long before us; James Brown funked up the stage not long before the building was razed in 1965. The dressing room was the smallest we had ever used for a concert since we had become recording artists. When we arrived to get changed there was no sign of Frankie or Bobby. Realistically we would have had to take turns using the room, but we did see George Hamilton IV before the show.

Looking back, it's hard to believe George was a teen idol before he became a country star in the Sixties. He was the next level of wholesome compared with his much more urban stagemates: reddy-brown neat hair, tall and skinny frame, quiet and courteous. Also not quite hitting the big time yet, George had, nonetheless, enjoyed some success in the upper reaches of the national charts with *A Rose and Baby Ruth* a year earlier. When we played

George Hamilton IV

Youngstown, he had recently released a second ballad, *Why Don't They Understand*, which would also make the Top Ten. George smiled sweetly at us as he donned his white sport coat (definitely not a tux) and fixed his red carnation, which may or may not have been a nod to his first hit. To an R&B vocal harmony group, these songs were boring as hell, however beautifully there were sung. But it didn't matter what we thought. George wouldn't be troubling these rock and roll shows for long, heading instead for Nashville and enormous country fame.

******

Frankie Avalon, by contrast, was on the brink of becoming the archetypal teen idol. He'd already been bubbling under for around five years, starting as a trumpet playing prodigy on TV, age 11, before being discovered as a potential singer by fellow Philadelphian Bob Marcucci, the young owner of Chancellor Records. Barely into his late twenties, Bob was also a lyricist and producer who would later work his marketing magic on another young 'sensation', Fabian. While our own Al Silver was a record industry guy through and through, Bob had the vision to exploit all possible channels for furthering the careers of his boys – not just music shows on TV, but supporting roles in movies. Frankie recorded mostly Bob's material at the time – an awesome manager, I have to say he was no Billy Myles or Bob Crewe when it came to songwriting – and before too long a very promising, small and cute package was put together that the parents of teenage girls wouldn't find too scary.

Bob and his business partner Peter DeAngelis needed a strong first hit for Frankie and they thought they had found it when they co-wrote *De De Dinah*, a piece of teen bubblegum that even those involved would admit wasn't their finest hour. Apparently Frankie pinched his nose while recording it to produce a nasal voice for fun, but it turned out to be the version that was released round the time we all played Youngstown. He also sang it on American Bandstand in the same month and it went on to sell a million, hitting #7 on the Billboard chart. To be honest, I can't remember if Frankie sang his surprise smash at the Elms Ballroom, but I do recall Eddie Quinn mimicking his nasal delivery as we all fell about laughing. Eddie had a gift for vocal impersonations, although they were often merciless. In any event, Frankie went down a storm that night and we were in no doubt that we were sharing a bill with a name to watch. His early days in groups, though not at first standing at the microphone, had taught him a good deal about stagecraft and he was already expert at working the crowd. In fact he had them wrapped around his finger.

These multi-artist shows in those days weren't long – certainly not the nearly three hour affairs that stadium filling rock stars have to deliver these days. Each artist would do two or three numbers which were separated by screaming and pushing from teenage fans, MCs waiting for the audience to calm down before introducing the next act, regular technical hitches, the late arrival of certain artists and delays in reaching the stage. Slick was not the word to describe most of the 100-plus gigs I played with the Mello-Kings while we were making records. The Elms Ballroom didn't lend itself to breaking this pattern. Since it was, well, a ballroom, the stage was almost at floor level, presumably designed for dance bands. This was far from ideal for vocal groups used to engaging with the crowd from a slight elevation which provided a useful barrier when audiences became overexcited. Also, there were no 'wings' offstage from which the other acts could watch us. They could either peer from the back of the hall, which would almost guarantee getting them spotted and chased by girls, or just miss the show until it was time to come on.

That night the house was packed; the vast majority were girls, in fact it's hard to remember any guys being there at all. We opened with *Do Baby Do*, which was followed by the usual messing about, then into *Tonite, Tonite*. During the second number a blonde right in front of us reached towards my leg and started unsnapping my shoe, wanting one of my prized white bucks for a souvenir. I managed to kick her hand away, but she was very persistent. Another girl kept interrupting us while we were singing.

"What's your name?" asked the girl, who seemed no more than a foot from my face. She was determined to have a full-on conversation in the middle of a show and get a response from each of us.

"My name's Neil," I replied with a smile.

Eddie wasn't at all pleased. "*My name's Neil!*" he mimicked in a whining voice while looking at me incredulously down the line – Bobby Scholl stood in front of us in the middle, with me and Larry on one side, Eddie and Jerry on the other. Eddie thought I was being unprofessional. He was right.

******

Bobby Darin (born Cassotto) was yet another Italian American whose career as a solo career was on the verge of really taking off after a couple of years of moderate success. Like the Mello-Kings, he was a New Yorker. Bobby had started out as a songwriter in the city's famous hit factory, the Brill Building, as well as working with Connie Francis (born Franconero – yes, I know, we get everywhere!), with whom he had an ill-fated romance before focusing on his singing. Aged 21 when we met him, Bobby was having a late bloom as a teen idol before progressing to be a polished performer of grown-up songs. *Splish Splash* – not a grown-up song by any definition, but a huge first hit for Bobby – didn't appear until several weeks after we played Youngstown. Up to that point he had been singing a wide range of songs; some, such as *Rock Island Line*, were traditional folk numbers brought up to date for young audiences, while others were self-penned originals. Maybe half a dozen of these had been released as non-charting singles. He drew on these to fill his slot at the Elms, but the girls didn't care, bowled over by his smile and easy charm. Three years later, while filming the movie *Come September*, Bobby deployed these to woo his gorgeous co-star Sandra Dee, who married him at 18. Lucky dog.

******

After we returned to the hotel, the Mello-Kings eventually dispersed to do their own thing. I stuck around, noticing a pool table in another area of the hotel's ground floor, and when Frankie and Bob suddenly showed up it was only natural that Avallone and Arena should shoot a few frames together. Bob followed Frankie around like the two of them were connected by a long piece of elastic. The manager didn't want to leave his young investment out of his sight for even a moment. Still, they were a good team and got on very well - Bob was, after all, still only 27 himself. I sensed at the time that it was a good relationship, which seemed to have remained the case for many years until Bob's death.

We played pool for a good 30 minutes, Bob literally standing over the table at each shot. He must have cut a strange figure in his $200 suit, looking every inch the metropolitan music big-shot in this unexceptional provincial hotel. We would have played for longer, had hunger not gotten the better of us. I reckon we had eaten nothing but candy all day. Soon the three of us were sitting down demolishing a mountain of spaghetti and meatballs – of course! Frankie and I were shooting the breeze easily. He was a cool kid and I enjoyed his company on that weekend. We talked about Philly, about Dick Clark having attended my high school in Mount Vernon, our respective experiences of Bandstand, that kind of thing. While we chatted, Bob combined eating with writing notes. I assume he was constantly jotting down business ideas as they came into his head; thoughts on where the careers of Frankie and his other young stars might go next. I don't think he'd been scribbling lyrics for new songs. If he had, I doubt they'd have been worse than the words to *De De Dinah.*

******

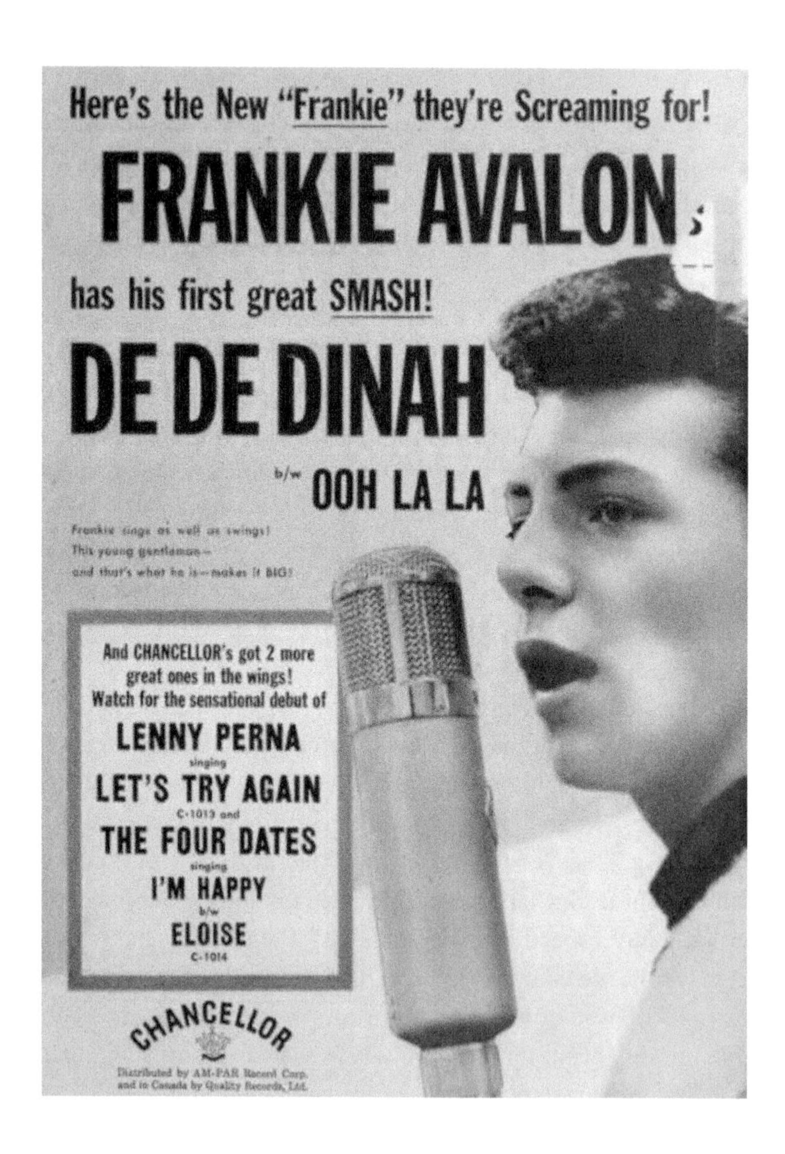
Here's the New "Frankie" they're Screaming for!
FRANKIE AVALON
has his first great SMASH!
DE DE DINAH
b/w OOH LA LA
Frankie sings as well as swings!
This young gentleman—
and that's what he is—makes it BIG!
And CHANCELLOR's got 2 more
great ones in the wings!
Watch for the sensational debut of
LENNY PERNA
singing
LET'S TRY AGAIN
C-1013 and
THE FOUR DATES
singing
I'M HAPPY
b/w
ELOISE
C-1014
CHANCELLOR
Distributed by AM-PAR Record Corp.
and in Canada by Quality Records, Ltd.

Soon after we awoke in Youngstown on the morning of Saturday 7 December, I got dressed and went downstairs on my own, only to see Bobby Darin sitting in the hotel lobby wearing a long gray winter coat. I caught his eye and, taking off his hat, he came over to greet me, shaking my hand warmly.

"You guys were great," he enthused. "I really loved your stuff. My name's Bobby Darin. You don't know me now, but you will."

With a smile, Bobby turned up his coat collar against the cold and turned to stride out of the hotel.

To this day, I still cherish that moment. I would even go as far as saying I was more thrilled to meet Bobby Darin than anyone else on our journey, even Jerry Lee Lewis. I became a huge fan as his career developed and even now, in my early 80s, I'm always pleased to be asked to sing one of his numbers if I'm doing a private show. *Beyond the Sea* is a firm a favourite of mine and it always reminds me of him singing among the audience on Dick Clark's 'Beech Nut' Show, picking out girls to dance with while expertly miming his famous hit.

I'm not sure how Bobby managed to catch any of our act in that terrible venue, but I've never forgotten what he said and have often reflected on it over the years: the curious mix of humility, generosity and absolute confidence. Some might have perceived it as arrogance, but Bobby was right to be sure of himself. His charm was perfectly genuine and his talent not for debate. His timing, phrasing and relaxed delivery when singing his best material would produce a swing to make Bennett, Martin and Sinatra proud. Bobby Darin was taken from us far too soon.

******

There had been snow overnight. Not a huge amount – about half an inch – but surprising since it seemed warmer than the previous day, in fact not that cold at all. It wasn't long before the snow melted to a nasty gray slush, spattering against the sides of the Mello-Bomb as I steered it carefully through the north of Mahoning County and on to route 80 to head east to New York City. My sister Marie had warned me not to return without Frankie Avalon's

Bobby Darin, 1957

autograph, a mission I failed to complete because he was nowhere to be seen when we left.

I returned to Youngstown a few times in the years that followed, not to sing but to drive my mom to visit Connie, who was widowed very young when her husband Tony died. Basil was Connie's brother and he stayed in Youngstown, raising eight children. I had always got on well with Basil: he was a little older than me and, when he was still a student at New Rochelle High School before moving west, he would regularly take me to basketball games.

Our Youngstown gigs had given me a lot to think about on the way home. We had been used to playing alongside several other groups on large 'package' tours, but this time we had been the only group sharing a bill with three solo guys. We were also a little younger on average than George, Frankie and Bobby. But more significantly, they were all in the process of reinventing themselves – as it happened, extremely successfully in all cases. I know it's hard for me to be unbiased, but I truly believe the Mello-Kings were a class act in anybody's book: our harmonies were second to none, in a style that had until us been almost exclusively the preserve of black groups; our performances were consistently as close to flawless as possible. Yet, successful and popular as we were, the group was singing on a very crowded stage. Changing direction would be difficult for a vocal-only group: our lack of instruments would make us, more often than not, dependant on a band or orchestra, since the charm of *a capella* had relatively limited appeal; a bunch of singers would also have limited scope for composition or even simply singing a new style of music. Our Youngstown co-stars each became very different kinds of solo singers, embracing a range of genres and complementing each pivot with movie appearances or even their own TV shows.

Anyway, there was still fun for me to have, our fans adored us and Christmas was just around the corner. “What’s not to like?” I concluded.

Chapter 13

Ain't That A Kick In The Head

THE William Morris Agency was arguably the most famous talent agency in the world. Founded in New York and later headquartered in Hollywood, WMA represented some of the best known 20th century entertainers in film, television and music – from Charlie Chaplin, Mae West and the Marx Brothers in the 1930s to the Rolling Stones and the Beach Boys in the 1960s, not to mention hundreds of famous authors. And the Mello-Kings. In theory, at least.

Between our Washington DC / Baltimore tour and the trip to Ohio, Al Silver told us that WMA wanted to meet us. A good contact of his had heard good things about us and thought he could take us to yet another level. We arrived on foot at the agency's swanky offices in Manhattan, wearing our white stage outfits to impress. Sometimes I wonder if we'd looked ridiculous walking through the streets of New York in broad daylight dressed for singing R&B on TV, but I guess nobody even noticed in those crazy days of showbiz teen sensations. We waited in reception, each of us staring wide-eyed at the endless rows of stars' pictures on the wall. Out of an office door came a long outstretched arm heading towards us, attached to a huge, preppy-looking guy in his late forties with a confident grin that was only very slightly insincere.

George Archer shook each of our hands vigorously, maintaining eye contact and his perma-smile as he told us what a pleasure it was to meet 'Al's boys'. We hung around for a while, making low-level conversation about what we'd been doing and where we'd been in recent months, before George swerved the meeting towards a swift conclusion.

"Here's what I want you to do: come for dinner at the Ardsley Club. Meet my friends. We'll have a lot of fun. I'm going to send a contract over to Al and I want you to sign it. You're going to be my five little Elvis Presleys."

It was a surreal meeting that seemed to raise more questions than answers. Was Irv Nahan not representing us anymore? Did WMA work with anyone else we had played alongside? Could this be the beginning of something really big?

The following week we all turned up at the Ardsley Country Club, an impossibly swanky establishment which, in those days, was still on the banks of the Hudson near Dobbs Ferry. Pulling up outside the 'English Tudor' building in the Mello Bomb, we quickly decided to park somewhere more discreet; we already felt uncomfortable and a little shabby, despite our efforts to look as neat and tidy as possible in our best jeans and polo-style shirts. It was one of the few occasions which required something between everyday teenage wear and our stage outfits. Announcing ourselves nervously at the desk, it was only a few seconds before our host appeared, his huge frame clad in an expensive looking sport coat, arms outstretched in a welcome that was warm, yet not too showy. "You made it! That's great!" enthused George. "Come on in!" He gestured towards what must have been the dining room, before realizing he should lead us in, turning every so often to smile

The Ardsley Country Club, Irvington

encouragingly and check we were still there. George's wife was already sitting at a beautifully laid out round table, waiting for us. Blonde, sort of attractive, younger. A trophy wife. He was no Don Juan.

"What a handsome bunch of guys – more handsome than in the photos," gushed Mrs Archer. 'I'm so glad my husband's handling you!" After beaming at each of us for a few seconds to reinforce her endorsement, I'm not sure she spoke again for the entire dinner. Urged by George to order anything we liked from the menu, we played it safe to avoid embarrassment, but it was all there: lobster, steak, you name it. We were surrounded by affluent people, some of them friends of George, and every so often during the evening he would introduce us to them as they passed by our table, no doubt curious as to why their fellow member was entertaining a group of kids from the wrong suburbs of New York.

For the rest of the dinner, George talked to us in very general terms about the music scene, what we hoped to achieve, who we admired, that kind of thing. As a career discussion, it wasn't really going anywhere, but we were having an OK time. It was a rare Saturday night when we didn't have a gig and were doing something a little different, with someone else paying. That said, we were acutely aware that we were out of our league in that place and knew exactly when to call it a night. We found a good time to make a reasonable excuse to be someplace else, said goodnight to Mrs Archer and thanked George for his hospitality.

We never saw him again.

******

A couple of months passed before there was any sign of WMA showing any interest in us. We were back from Youngstown and the end of 1957 was in sight. *Sassafrass* hadn't been a huge hit, although it was a popular live number and, thankfully, nobody seemed as down on the record as the Mello-Kings themselves. Bookings for anything worthwhile seemed to be slowing down, with no more major 'package' tours on the horizon. It was probably just a natural lull; a pause in the momentum of our workload. The Mello-Kings had been marching to the relentless beat of increasing demand for the whole of the year, so this felt alien to us and our youth, unsurprisingly, made us impatient.

We reluctantly agreed to a gig set up by Irv at Michigan State University at East Lansing, which involved a 10 hour drive and a distance approaching 700 miles from Mount Vernon. It sounds unbelievable when you think how easy it would be to fly nowadays; all the more incredible considering how cars were less reliable in the Fifties. Even so, the Mello Bomb rose to the occasion and completed the round trip without any trouble. Our very early start left us with plenty of time, particularly since we were the last act in an evening show that was scheduled to finish relatively late. The unforeseen element of our timetable, however, was the apparent refusal of the preceding act to leave the stage.

Joni James was a striking brunette, and an Italian American like me – her birth name was Giovanna Babbo. She had already enjoyed a string of hits over five years, starting with the chart-topping *Why Don't You Believe Me?* in 1952, which was swiftly followed by a successful cover of Hank Williams's *You're Cheatin' Heart*. After finding fame beyond the US and winning a number of awards, it was a little surprising that she was working the college circuit. In any event, she was given the full star treatment by the organisers, who made sure she was driven the unusually long distance from the off-theater dressing room to backstage, while we had to walk in the cold December evening, dodging puddles in our white shoes. Joni was perhaps a little 'traditional' for a student crowd more familiar with rock and roll; her beautiful white gown and repertoire of ballads sung in her distinctive vibrato might have seemed somewhat out of place among the blue jeans and letterman jackets. Even so, she wowed the audience with hit after hit in a set lasting almost two hours. She just wouldn't get off stage and nobody was calling time on her marathon performance.

Our greatest worry was that it was getting late in the evening and the crowd was already starting to disperse before we'd even started. We weren't, however, prepared for the *prima donna* behavior that followed. Eventually coming down the steps off the stage, aware that the evening was beginning to wind down even though there was another act to go, Joni James looked at us and simply said: "Now see if you can follow that – fuck you, Mello-Kings."
Eddie and I looked at each other, before replying, "Same to you!"
What did this 26 year old, established, successful, married woman

Joni James

have against a group of young guys? She didn't even know us and we'd done nothing wrong.

We went on stage, performed at least 10 songs and made the best of a shitty situation, but the trip had been a terrible waste of time. More than half the crowd had gone home. It felt like a real low point, but sometimes that's just showbusiness. Ordinarily, there might have been a silver lining and Michigan was poised to deliver. Seeing our disappointment and frustration, a stage hand walked to us and said: "Don't worry guys, we've got five hot chicks waiting for you back at the clubhouse." But it wasn't to be. We were already committed to a late drive after the show so that we could get a head start on the next day, when we had a small gig on the way home.

******

Al Silver had us doing promotions all over the place. I was recently asked how many TV and radio appearances we made during the time we were recording in 1957 (remember, a number of songs were laid down in the studio, but didn't emerge for up to three years afterwards, either for the first time or as reissues). After trying to add it up, I'm guessing well over a hundred, since they were at least a couple of times a week, with more than one on some days. Although the records were selling further afield, school commitments – in theory, at least – for most of us meant we had to concentrate our travelling efforts on cities in the north eastern states. The distances between some of these places was still huge: Detroit to Boston to the Carolinas and back to New York made for some punishing schedules.

One of the worst of these was a weekend in Boston: despite the five of us staying in the city's very swanky Hotel Touraine, furnished like a French chateau, the radio work took place on one of the Boston Harbour Islands, where the studio was located next to a large transmitter. We went backwards and forwards to the from city to island, as dictated by the demands of live radio programming in those days. It was extremely tedious and we saw nobody except the DJ and a studio engineer.

Others at least brought us into contact with fellow performers, which by the end of 1957 were a much more varied group than the usual crowd of R&B vocal groups or wild rock and rollers. Mel Tillis was one such artist. Meeting George Hamilton on the Youngstown bill had added a country angle for the first time in one of our shows and, different again, Mel was starting out as a writer and singer of early country-rock. A neat, slender fellow from Florida, Mel literally wore his country roots on his sleeve with a fondness for fancy embroidery on his jackets. Like our old friends the Del-Vikings, he had spent time in the US Air Force, but had left the service with much better manners.

We were hanging around in yet another TV studio waiting area when Mel strolled over to introduce himself, acoustic guitar dangling neck-down on his back.

"Hey guys, how're you doin'? I'm M-m-m-Mel T-t-t-Tillis. G-g-g-good to m-m-m-eeeeeet you!"

We hadn't been prepared for Mel's stutter, which certainly didn't feature in his singing; it was apparently a lasting effect of having caught malaria as a child. Normally this kind of surprise would have started Eddie giggling, but thankfully he just stared instead, possibly sharing my thoughts: why didn't Mel just avoid difficult words like those? Anyway, we liked the guy and enjoyed watching him through the studio window when he sang *Juke Box Man*, a fun number with a rocky beat which he'd released a few months before.

By way of great contrast, also performing in the studio that day was the formidable jazz and gospel singer Della Reese. A year earlier, Della had recorded a cover of *In the Still of the Night*, the smash hit by our Al Silver stablemates, The Five Satins. She was riding high with the single *And That Reminds Me* when we saw her. The song always resonated with me because it was based on the old Italian instrumental, *Concerto d'autunno*. We didn't get to chat with Della that day, but she was a class act.

MEL TILLIS

If You'll Be My Love b/w

Juke Box Man

4—40944-c

It was inevitable that, sooner or later, the promotions schedule would get out of control and that we'd be sent on a wild goose chase. This one was a mere 400 mile round trip to Delaware, where we were supposed to be sharing a bill with the Jesters and the Paragons. We drove for hours only to find that the promoter had messed up the dates and there was nobody at the theater, apart from the three singing groups. The consolation was that we got to hang out with a great bunch of guys. The Jesters and the Paragons were more than label mates on Paul Winley Records; they were effectively brother groups. Both from Harlem, they were classic products of the street corner doo wop scene – which was much more interesting to us than rock and roll or bubblegum pop. Winley, an early member of the Brill Building songwriting team, had discovered both groups (the Jesters at an Apollo amateur night) and was doing a good job delivering a string of releases for them. None was a smash, but all were well followed in the north eastern states. A couple of years after we met them, Winley released *The Paragons Meet The Jesters*, a successful album which had packaged to suggest a doo wop showdown between the 'rivals'.

The Jesters, in particular, were keen to sing in some way after their own long, abortive journey. It was a way of keeping the mood light, when in reality we were all pretty pissed. Expert at finding weird locations with good acoustics, the five Jesters headed for the men's bathroom in the theatre, followed by the five Mello-Kings. Some might have said that the black group was the real deal and the white guys were just pretenders, but we enjoyed each other's company and there was a lot of mutual respect in that bathroom as we traded harmonies and improvised on songs from both sides, as well as some other favourites. And of course, the lavatorial acoustics were great! Back in New York, Irv apologised for the mistake and assured us we'd get paid anyway. We never did.

In the same few weeks, we were summoned to a brownstone in Brooklyn to meet the yet-to-be-famous DJ and promoter, Murray the K. Already in his mid-30s, Murray Kaufman had enjoyed a successful career as a promoter and record plugger since leaving the US Army. The phenomenal energy and enthusiasm he injected into all his projects eventually took him to New York radio stations WMCA and WMGM, which was where he got to hear about the Mello-Kings. Convinced we were a black doo-wop act and refusing to believe otherwise, Murray asked Al Silver to send us round to his house; we could sing him a couple of numbers and prove the color of our faces. While this sounded like a ridiculous exercise, Murray was starting to build a good following for his live shows and there were useful bookings to be had. Al also had another single release lined up for us, so this kind of thing couldn't do any harm. In fact Murray had already booked us for a gig at Palisades Park, the huge amusement park in New Jersey, directly across the Hudson from Upper Manhattan. His series of shows at the park became very popular and, before he moved on to his 'big break' all-night radio show at WINS, prepared the ground for those hosted in the same location by star DJs Clay Cole and 'Cousin Brucie' Morrow as the Fifties became the Sixties.

Murray sat in an armchair, examining us up and down as we stood before him, an alien species: the white doo wop group. He was wearing his trademark straw hat indoors. In late 1957 it must have been a recent purchase – we hadn't seen it before, but it became a permanent fixture. We sang *Tonite, Tonite,* after which he simply said: "Yeah, yeah, that's great. Thanks for dropping by. See you at the show." Perhaps he was a little embarrassed about his curiosity, but it was no big deal to us.

The other 'Bandstand' TV show we appeared on in the run-up to Christmas was Ted Steele's. While Dick Clark was building his powerbase from Philadelphia, Ted, a 40 year old former band-

Murray the K

leader, was reaching teenagers through his broader based variety show on New York's WOR-TV (Channel 9). Ted Steele's Bandstand gave Bill Haley and his Comets one of their first major TV appearances in 1955. It was an important show and we were delighted to be invited on to exactly the sort of programme that our families and friends might watch, although perhaps it wasn't as cool as our slots with Dick Clark. *Sassafrass* was treading water in the charts, so we opted for the crowd-pleasing combo of *Tonite, Tonite* and *Do Baby Do*. Most of the individual segments of this Bandstand were introduced by a young woman, following the now familiar format of individual namechecks for the group and a few encouraging comments to the viewers at home.

"Hey girls, this group has some good looking, fair-haired Irish boys; dark-haired, handsome Italian boys; they're all here in the Mello-Kings!"

Walking down the line to speak briefly to each of us, our short-haired lady interviewer lingered a little longer with Bobby; he was very popular. "See, girls?" she drooled into the camera when she'd finished with the small talk, "They are *handsome*!"

******

Al Silver was a great planner and left no stone unturned when it came to supporting new releases with promotional performances, interviews or gimmicks to raise our profile. Encouraged by the hefty mailbags that arrived at Herald after our Dick Clark appearance, Al had thought that a Christmas card for Mello-Kings fans might be a good way of keeping us front-of-mind with record buyers. Our single *Baby Tell Me Why, Why, Why* would be released at the beginning of December, so the timing was good. In reality, it was too much hassle for Al's small team: organising photographers, distribution to retail outlets, mailing lists for fans; there just wasn't time. He came up with a better idea that would take seconds – we would record a jingle for radio stations to pay between records. "*The Mello-Kings Wish You A Merry Christmas!*" A few takes of singing some nonsense into a microphone and we'd be all done. So that's what we did.

Many years later, sometime in the Seventies, I was reminded of the Christmas card by my childhood friend Ralph Castaldo. I must digress to tell you about him, because he was one of my more colourful friends outside of the music business and we had a lot of fun times together since meeting at the age of five. Ralph's grandparents owned two houses next to each other on S 9th Avenue, where I lived. An only child, Ralph was doted on by his parents: his mother was beautiful and always well turned out; his father worked for a gravestone company where, towards the end of his career, he had a bad fall and severed a finger. Ralph was the first boy at school to have blue suede shoes. On his 16th birthday his dad gave him a canary-yellow Pontiac Convertible with a red interior. I guess we all knew someone like that when we were teenagers. No wonder Dolores Ianello, a girl at school, asked me to introduce them. Ralph would pick me up from home and we'd double date in the Pontiac, me with Mary Ann, him with Dolores. They were eventually married.

Back to my Seventies phone call from Ralph: it was around Christmas time and he had been in Greenwich Village with Dolores. They were in a store that sold Christmas cards and there it was, with five festive faces grinning from the photograph on the front– *"The Mello-Kings Wish You A Merry Christmas!"*. Ralph was calling me from his house in Pelham and urged me to come and see the card. It was a clearly a fake. I can't imagine the supplier to the store would have sold many at a time when New York was heavily into disco and punk, but collectively we managed to track him down. Assisted by a letter from a golfing acquaintance and lawyer, Bohn Vergari, son of the famous Westchester County District Attorney, Carl, I was compensated for the lack of permission when reproducing my image for an unauthorised product.

December progressed, eventually bringing an unexpected phone call from George Archer. After several weeks, if not months of radio silence, he had secured possibly the most significant opportunity of our career since playing the Apollo: an audition for the Ed Sullivan Show.

In practice, usually just a rubber-stamping of artistes before booking them for a date on the show, the audition wasn't held at the theatre but at a large Manhattan office fitted with a glass-screened performance space. We were shown into a long, empty room by a casually dressed young man with a clipboard. On the other side of the glass was a sleek, well-coiffured blonde, not outstandingly

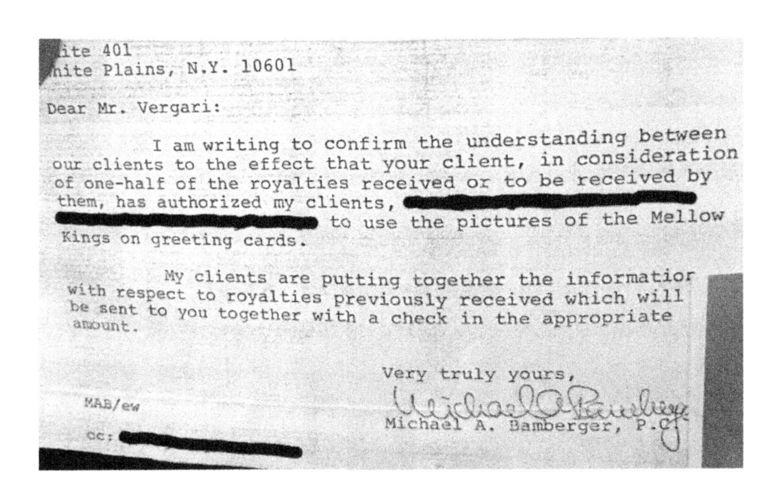

ite 401
hite Plains, N.Y. 10601

Dear Mr. Vergari:

I am writing to confirm the understanding between our clients to the effect that your client, in consideration of one-half of the royalties received or to be received by them, has authorized my clients, [redacted] to use the pictures of the Mellow Kings on greeting cards.

My clients are putting together the informatior with respect to royalties previously received which will be sent to you together with a check in the appropriate amount.

Very truly yours,

Michael A. Bamberger, P.C.

MAB/ew

cc: [redacted]

beautiful, but serious looking and clearly a decision maker. She moved her perfectly made-up face towards a hole in the screen.

"Go ahead kids." A woman of few words.

We sang *Tonite, Tonite – a capella –* which guaranteed a flawless performance and an opportunity to showcase harmonies that, heard up close, would make this steely dame shiver. She returned to the hole.

"Thanks for coming in."

What the fuck? As we stood there looking at each other with a mixture of embarrassment and confusion, a second guy, this time better dressed in a gray flannel suit, ran in on the other side of the glass and talked to her briefly. We assumed he worked for George Archer and had been sent to watch the audition. Back to the hole.

"Can you do something else?"

Sensing that the blonde needed to be blown away by something that was a little more 'grown up', we opted for *Moonlight in Vermont.* The uniquely harmonised arrangement that Levister had worked up for us sounded incredible in that rehearsal room. Jerry had a high note at the end that used to make audiences gasp with pleasure when we were doing those early club gigs. The folks behind the glass screen were doing the same.

"That was perfect, you'll hear from us."

We left those Ed Sullivan offices under the firm impression that we would be called by somebody with a large diary. We would have reached the summit.

Walking back to the elevator, each with a spring in his step, we pressed the button and waited. We could already hardly speak with excitement, but when the elevator doors opened we were truly lost for words. Standing alone in the middle of the cabin was Dean Martin. My idol. Dean was wearing a beautifully cut dark brown suit, with a tie to match and dark brown shoes that were so clean and shiny you could eat off them. I was the first Mello-King to enter the elevator, turning 180 degrees to stand alongside Dean. The others followed and assembled around him in an orderly, respectful fashion. I was so nervous that I found myself standing on one leg, like a flamingo. Dean looked sideways at me. Perhaps he was mildly curious about our white outfits, complete with Larry's 'M-logo' on the white jacket.

If there was ever a moment in my life when I wanted desperately to turn back the clock and do or say something different, that's it. I would have shaken Dean Martin's hand, introduced myself and the others, talked about the audition - anything that might have made him remember us, at least vaguely, and taken us seriously as fellow artists. Or we could have used the stunt we'd employed so many times, mainly around girls, to show off our harmonies: suddenly breaking into song with Dean's name, each of us chiming in with an impressive new layer to end with five stunning, contrasting frequencies. Dean, Dean, Deeeaaaan! In the elevator.

We got to the bottom and I walked out first with Dean. We all remained silent. As he walked he dipped coolly into his suit pocket to pull out his cigarettes. Pausing to light up, he walked directly ahead as he exited the building and crossed the street, smoking. We all turned right.

The Ed Sullivan Show always filled its schedule many weeks in advance. They never called.

Chapter 14

All good things

The end of the road for the original Mello-Kings was in December 1957. Two months later, only three remained from the quintet formed by Levister. Contrary to a number of accounts written in subsequent years, I wasn't the first to leave: it was Larry.

There was a lot of sitting around during the endless wait to hear from the Ed Sullivan Show. As Christmas week approached, it felt that while the unstoppable express train of pop music was gathering yet more speed, we were hanging on to the back, waiting to be shaken off at the next bend. Package tours were evolving into shows with a much greater variety of artists and, apart from a booking to appear briefly once or twice locally on a long tour in January with the Everly Brothers, Buddy Holly and Eddie Cochran, there wasn't much on the horizon. Our own Eddie was getting interested in songwriting and we still had some recorded material ready to go, but it was quiet. Irv Nahan was dealing with a revolving door in the Drifters, which had become a potentially major business opportunity for him; Al Silver, meanwhile, was busy recording new acts that were taking him beyond his usual blues and R&B – Gene Ross, Ronnie Pearson, Charlie & Ray, among others.

Our single *Baby Tell Me Why, Why, Why* was failing to set the charts alight. I thought it was a pretty good song, as was its flip side, *The Only Girl*, which Eddie had written with Levister. Sensibly wanting to cash in on the growing album market, while showcasing his widening range of recording talent, Al Silver released a compilation in December 1957 called *Herald the Beat*. Featuring three tracks from us alongside Faye Adams, the Turbans, the Nutmegs, Al Savage and Tommy Ridgeley, the LP once featured in a review of the worst cover sleeves. I can't say it was unfair, since it showed a guy in a red Robin Hood style outfit blowing a long horn (as would a herald) at a young woman who was standing back in a state of badly posed shock.

Larry is four years older than me. Obviously not a high school teen star, in the early days of the Mellotones and Mello-Kings he had been working various jobs including using his artistic talent at Terrytoons Inc, the famous animation studio in New Rochelle. Larry had always hated life on the road as a musician, he had trouble sleeping and eventually it would catch up with him as he struggled to keep awake at important times – like when he was driving us back from a gig and I had to grab the wheel after a wild swerve that could have killed us all. It was another change of direction, without warning, that he sprang on us while were sitting around in our usual rehearsals in the boys club.

Something was clearly up. Thinking as he was speaking, Larry began to ramble nervously, shifting uneasily, dropping his head and looking at his feet. He was winding up his punch.

"I'm older than you guys…There isn't much happening right now…We're not getting the money we're supposed to…" and so it went on until we were left in no doubt that our friend was serious and wouldn't change his mind.

Our hearts had been ripped from our chests. I felt sick. Perhaps, despite the lack of bookings at the end of 1957, the rest of us hadn't

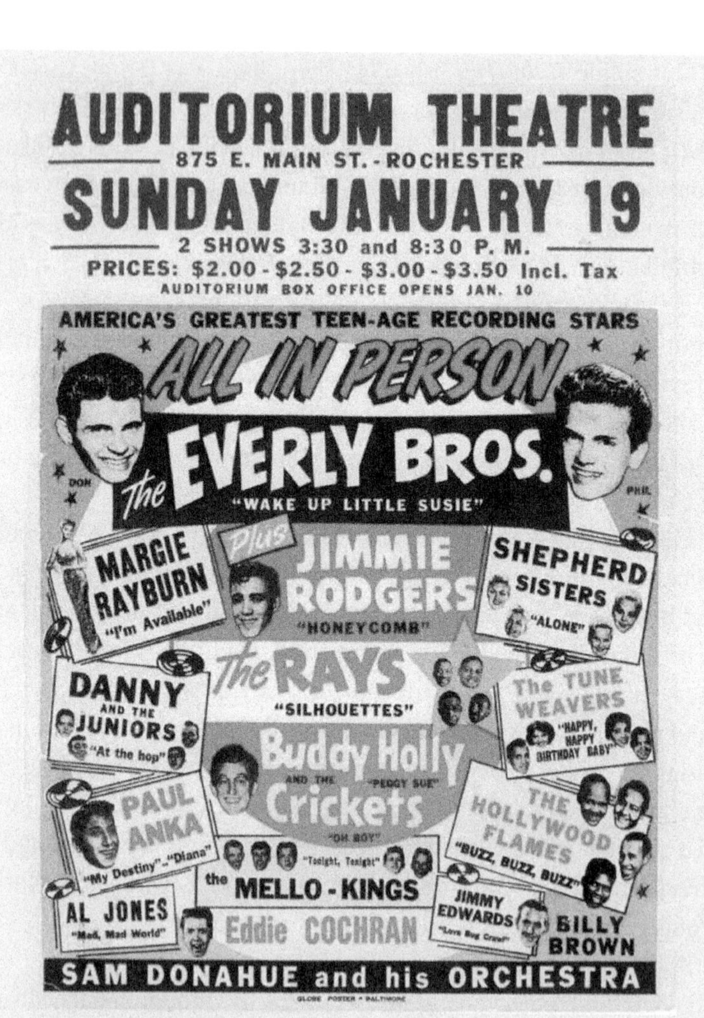
AUDITORIUM THEATRE
875 E. MAIN ST. - ROCHESTER
SUNDAY JANUARY 19
2 SHOWS 3:30 and 8:30 P. M.
PRICES: $2.00 - $2.50 - $3.00 - $3.50 Incl. Tax
AUDITORIUM BOX OFFICE OPENS JAN. 10
AMERICA'S GREATEST TEEN-AGE RECORDING STARS
ALL IN PERSON
DON
PHIL
The EVERLY BROS.
"WAKE UP LITTLE SUSIE"
MARGIE RAYBURN
"I'm Available"
Plus
JIMMIE RODGERS
"HONEYCOMB"
SHEPHERD SISTERS
"ALONE"
DANNY AND THE JUNIORS
"At the hop"
The RAYS
"SILHOUETTES"
The TUNE WEAVERS
"HAPPY, HAPPY BIRTHDAY BABY"
Buddy Holly AND THE Crickets
"PEGGY SUE"
"OH BOY"
PAUL ANKA
"My Destiny" - "Diana"
THE HOLLYWOOD FLAMES
"BUZZ, BUZZ, BUZZ"
"Tonight, Tonight"
the MELLO - KINGS
AL JONES
"Mad, Mad World"
Eddie COCHRAN
JIMMY EDWARDS
"Love Bug Crawl"
BILLY BROWN
SAM DONAHUE and his ORCHESTRA

lost hope. The alternative was school, which would have to be finished at some point, but for the time being we still believed we were invincible rock and roll stars. I can't speak for the others, but my own sense of loss was focused on what a waste it would be to break up the Mello-Kings. We were a perfect five part set up and Larry's rich, low voice worked beautifully in the group. The elaborate and painstakingly rehearsed harmonies just wouldn't – and couldn't – be the same without him. His vocal range was phenomenal, from bass to falsetto; even Dick Clark had noticed it.

"Are you sure this is right? We can't replace you." We kept saying this, in turn, over and over again, each time knowing it would be a fruitless effort.

"I'm sure you can find another bass," Larry said, more than once.

"Where? And who? Someone who has to learn all the songs from the beginning? We've already done all the groundwork and moved on. Everybody wants to be a Mello-King, but it doesn't mean they'd fit."

We didn't rehearse that night.

******

The next morning the four of us and Levister met at the Lincoln Lounge to discuss next steps. We couldn't give up on the group, however slow things had become in those few weeks. There was too much at stake because we'd then be drawing a final line under the opportunity that the dedication, hard work, endless hours of rehearsing and thousands of miles on the road had begun to turn into a reality over more than a year. So we agreed to carry on and find another bass. In the meantime, rehearsals started again and I carried the whole of the necessary lower register with my baritone. If Levister had adjusted the harmonies so that I could drop down just a little, I could have alternated between both parts and we might

have carried on indefinitely as a four piece. We tried and we performed as such in January: it was fine, but it just wasn't the same. Several guys auditioned for the bass job, perhaps eight or nine. I didn't think any of them were even nearly as good as Larry. Whoever we might have found eventually, as far as I was concerned it wasn't going to work out.

"This is going nowhere," I said in the next rehearsal. I was now making the same speech as Larry, standing in the same spot. The guys were speechless, but not as shocked as they had been only a little while before. I guess the second punch never hurts as much as the first.

"I don't know if I'm making the right decision, but I've had enough."

That could have been the end of the Mello-Kings forever.

******

Eddie called a few weeks later. He wanted me to go and see the group at a small gig in Yonkers. He had recruited Tony Pinto, the brother of a girl he was seeing at the time, to replace me as a fourth member. I'm not sure why I went; maybe it was out of my fondness for Eddie, or maybe it was just plain curiosity. I've been asked more recently if it was painful to see them perform without me that day. The answer is, of course, yes, although my pain was possibly outweighed by the depressing spectacle of a 60% original Mello-King group playing in a shithole club, making a perfectly passable sound, without even a hint of the magic that had existed barely two months before. When I left to go home, I was completely satisfied that quitting the group had been the right thing to do.

******

My friends in the group, as well as others I hung out with, had almost all grown up with not very much. In February 1958 I expected that most of the colour in my life was about to drain away – and I wasn't wrong. I went back to A.B. Davis, where I'd started four years earlier with every intention of going to college afterwards, helped by my sporting talent; who knows, I might have even been in line for a scholarship. However, my music commitments had forced me to quit some of the more academically rigorous subjects and I'd fallen behind in others. From having an early gift for math, I found myself taking some real 'Mickey Mouse' classes, mainly around low-level business administration. My goal was simply to graduate, so I sucked it up and kept my head down, at least most of the time. I returned to playing basketball and effectively swapped being a mainly absent teenage rock and roll star for the life of a typical high school jock. I graduated, as planned, the following year.

Over that same period, the Mello-Kings recruited a fifth member, Louis Jannacone. In the same month I left, *Tonite, Tonite* saw a revival in interest, presumably a result of expanded radio play. Herald re-released the song on an Extended Play 45 with *She's Real Cool*, *The Only Girl* and *Do Baby Do*. It was followed in spring 1958 by *Valerie*, co-written by Paul Evans, who later recorded *Seven Little Girls Sitting In The Back Seat*. In January 1959, the same Mello-Kings line up released *Chip Chip*, by Eddie Quinn and Levister, but by the time I finally left A.B. Davis, Eddie had also decided to quit. He took a job at the Copacabana, while continuing to write songs and attempting a solo singing career as 'Kevin McQuinn'.

Fielding only the Scholl Brothers as originals, the group pressed on for less than two more years, releasing a couple of low-selling singles and appearing on some compilations. Bobby left for military service, eventually rejoining the same line-up to tour again. Several personnel changes followed, with only Jerry remaining the original member by the mid-1970s. Four years after Larry and I left, we reunited with Eddie and the Scholls in Jerry's basement to talk about recovering royalties we believed were owed to us from that heyday of 1957. An attorney was instructed and set on a wild goose chase to follow the money. Our story was apparently typical of pop groups from the Fifties through the Nineties: towards the end of that

Back at school, collecting my third Most Valued Player trophy

long period, songwriters and their publishers had most of the power; when sales of physical recorded music began to slow, the valuable commodity was the song itself. Concerts and touring used to promote records; now, in the age of streaming, and easy or free access to music, it's the other way round. Eddie had co-written one or two of the Mello-Kings' records with Levister, but our biggest hit had been written solely by Billy Myles who, in the mid-Fifties, would possibly have been paid a fixed and final fee for the song, leaving the publisher holding the value.

On several occasions we were told that the record company had paid for hotels, drivers, promotional activity and much else that had to be netted against record sales, hence the limited final returns spread among five singers. I know this will come as sad news for my lifelong fiend Mike D'Angelo, who for decades has been convinced I've been hiding a large stash of Mello-Kings earnings under my mattress. There are plenty of stories, amusing and appalling, of huge rock bands touring the world, flying by Concorde, staying in (and trashing) fancy hotels and putting all the booze and drugs on expenses, only to be handed a long invoice at the end of the year alongside a smaller royalty check.

Herald's success had peaked with Maurice Williams and the Zodiacs reaching Number One with *Stay* in 1960. It coincided with the 'payola' investigations up to 1962, where the IRS and other federal agencies were lifting the lid on the practice of record companies paying commercial radio stations to play songs without the station disclosing the income. Faced with huge tax bills across the Herald, Ember and Angel publishing businesses, Al Silver opted to liquidate and pay creditors who had helped him build his business, rather than seek protection through bankruptcy. The move required him to lease his publishing catalogue for twenty years, but he later told music industry commentators that he regretted it deeply and should have let the record company go instead. Al effectively quit the frontline of showbiz and moved to Florida. He was a tough boss, but many were far tougher and less scrupulous. Ultimately, I have no reason to believe Al Silver was dishonorable in his dealings with the Mello-Kings.

******

If going back to A.B. Davis had brought me back to earth with a thud after my taste of rock and roll life, being at home was even worse. Business had been tough for my Dad and the bank foreclosed on our house. We moved to 1 Willow Place, a little further north in Mount Vernon and made the best of it. After I graduated, my lack of direction, relatively limited options outside the long shot of returning to music, and my love of sport took me

It Looks Like The
1st 1,000,000 For
EMBER RECORDS

The ORIGINAL Hit!

Billy Myles'

"THE JOKER"

Ember 1026

- - - - - - - - - -

Coming Up Strong!

The 5 Satins

"OUR ANNIVERSARY"

Ember 1025

- - - - - - - - - -

The Tonight Tonight **Mello Kings**

Do It Again With . . .

"SASSAFRASS"

H-507

- - - - - - - - - -

EMBER - HERALD RECORDS
1697 Broadway
New York 19, New York

to the Rockrimmon Country Club at North Stamford. There I worked in the pro shop and met several famous members. Benny Goodman, who once turned up with Hoagy Carmichael, was a cheap tipper - even after I adjusted his wood until my fingers bled.

I must have been 21 when I decided I should think about doing something meaningful with my earnings, such as they were, from the Mello-Kings. Having been paid OK money from some of the larger package tours, plus some royalties from record sales over a relatively short period, after some modest squandering in line with my youthful tastes I still had $3,000 in my bank account – worth around $32,000 in 2022. Mom had the bank book, but when I asked her for it she said she hadn't seen it for long time. Later she broke down and showed me there was only $7.77 in the account. My parents had needed the money. My dad had lost everything. What could I say?

Mindful that I never wanted to be in that situation, and perhaps thinking that one day I might even be able to help my older family on to a more secure footing, I took an opportunity to pursue a career in insurance and made a good living until I retired. I gained some great friends and clients along the way, supported and raised my kids, and kept aside enough time to keep my interest in music alive.

The first of the Mello-Kings to pass away was Bobby in 1975. He was killed in a boating accident while scuba diving at Long Island. It was always a mystery to me why he had even been there, when he could have indulged his leisure interest nearer to home. I kept in touch with Eddie, whose nieces were friends with my daughter, Rosemarie. He remained in the hospitality business until he sadly died in California in 2006. At his funeral, Jerry told me the cause had been an asthma attack. In the Seventies, Eddie would call me from the west coast in the middle of the night while he was smoking weed. He usually wanted me to hear a song he'd just written. The guy was a one-off and I still miss him very much.

Weed and asthma were possibly a bad combination. For many years there was something about my regular contact with Eddie that puzzled me. Before he moved west he would visit me in my office every so often, just to shoot the breeze. He would keep asking me, with a slightly guilty tone, if I was 'doing OK'. I could only imagine he was referring to my health, my ongoing happiness or my bank balance. I was fine on all fronts, but when someone keeps raising it, you can't help feeling they know something you ought to, but don't.

Jerry died at his home in Yonkers in 2019. He had continued to tour with the Mello-Kings for more than 60 years, bringing in new, younger singers from time to time (realistically, they couldn't have been older). I'm not sure if that was his main business, but they seemed pretty active on the retro circuit at the time of his passing. Jerry's business partner, Mick Mansueto, still tours with the official new version of the group and is doing a great job keeping the music alive. Mick has, in recent years, invited me to sing with them. My days of doing the splits on stage are over, but I wish the guys well as they carry the torch. Dear Larry, our oldest colleague, is still with us at the time of writing. We try to stay in touch, along with our mutual friend and Edison *alumna*, Marjorie 'Pinky' Baird, who was always a great supporter of ours.

******

I have been truly blessed in many ways: family, friends, happiness and relatively good health, with the scoreboard still running, are all I could have ever hoped for; who would have thought that a chance meeting with Frank Piccininni in the hallway at school, 66 years ago, would have given me the greatest bonus of all, a rare opportunity that even now remains part of my everyday life.

Tonite, Tonite alone has turned out to mean so much to so many – memories of a first dance, first date, wedding song, or perhaps seeing the Mello-Kings singing live in one of the big auditoriums or small clubs. Old fans, and believe it or not, new ones, try to track me or Larry down every now and again; they want memorabilia signed or simply to recount a story about the old days, prompted by hearing our most famous number on the radio. What's more, these kind folks get in touch from all over the world, from Australia to Austria.

It's been many years since I moved from New York to settle in north Virginia, not far from DC. For more than two decades, much of my time in retirement has been spent working in various guises at the beautiful Belmont Country Club in Ashburn. Far from making my fingers bleed, the staff and members there are very quick to celebrate "old Neil's cool past as a rock and roller" and I've been invited to sing more often, and probably for longer, than I deserve. I never stopped completely after the Mello-Kings, occasionally performing in a small gig or in private, and I'll keep on singing – even if it's only in the shower - for as long as I still have enough breath. Sharing my voice has been a privilege.

Epilogue

2019

Tonite, Tonite is blasting from the speakers at the Westchester County Center in White Plains, NY, just as it might have done more than 60 years earlier. The song perhaps fits better with the pristine Art Deco exterior of the beautiful 5,000 seat multipurpose arena than with the state-of-the-art sporting facilities inside. The Center, which opened in 1930, was designed by architects Stewart Walker and Leon Gillette, who also created Rye Playland along New York's Long Island Sound. Pianist Percy Grainger played at the Center's opening concert. In the decades that followed, audiences have been treated to performances by such greats as Judy Garland, Liza Minnelli, Joan Sutherland, James Brown, Kenny Rogers, Janis Joplin, John Sebastian, Jimi Hendrix and The Who, alongside sporting spectacles such as the Harlem Globetrotters and World Wrestling Entertainment.

The Mello-Kings and I never performed at the Center. Now it's best known as the home of the Westchester Knicks, a professional basketball team of the NBA G League and the exclusive NBA Development League affiliate of the New York Knickerbockers. The Knicks play all 25 home games at the Center, which is only ten minutes from the team's practice facility in Greenburgh.

The Center is also a regular hang-out of Robert 'Diz' Di Fiore, a varsity baseball coach, former basketball mascot and now a public address announcer and musical coordinator at Section 1 basketball tournaments. A colourful character who has, in his own right, become an attraction at local games, Diz - sometimes known as 'DJ Dizzy Dog' - has an encyclopaedic knowledge of both basketball and pop music. His playlist is eclectic and, although you'd think an audience would want to be fired up with fist-pumping heavy rock, it features several easy listening favourites for the older crowd of workers in the arena. One of those is my friend Howie Green. What started out as a special request from Howie to play *Tonite, Tonite* is now, without fail, the very first number played by Diz before players are allowed to touch a basketball at the 20-minute mark during warmups. Sometimes Howie has called me up when the song is playing. It's a different sort of reminder for me. I did, in fact, play at the Center while in the Mello-Kings – but in shorts and carrying a ball during my two-year stint of varsity basketball, which I juggled with performing on the stage and graduating high school. In later years I would officiate games in Section 1. It's been a thrill to know that the guys at Westchester care that much about me to still play the song and associate it with my officiating on that floor.

2022

Diz, a former mascot for the WNBA's New York Liberty and the New York Islanders ice hockey team, says he'll continue the tradition he has started for as long he's in charge of the music. Who knows how long that will be? He may decide to pack up his playlist or, perish the thought, get replaced by some dude playing Bon Jovi. The Westchester County Center has been out of commission for two years because of the Covid pandemic and used instead as both a testing facility and vaccine center. Public games will recommence, initially, at Yorktown High School, some way upstate in Yorktown Heights.

Diz says he plans to play the song before the first game.

Picture Credits

Chapter 1

Grimes Elementary School
Courtesy of the Westchester County Historical Society

Neil Arena and Gabriel Albero
Neil Arena

Gemma and Augie Arena
Neil Arena

Chapter 2

AB Davis High School
Courtesy of the Westchester County Historical Society

Turn Hall
Courtesy of the Westchester County Historical Society

Jimmy Jones and the Pretenders
Rama Records

Chapter 3

Al Silver at the record press
Ellen Silver Stange

Billy Myles
Cash Box / Ember Records

Bob Crewe, Frank Slay and The Rays
Bob Crewe Foundation

Tonite, Tonite label
Neil Arena

Chapter 4

Apollo flyer
Larry Esposito

Varetta Dillard
Groove /RCA Records

Earl Bostic
King Records / Collectables Records

Chapter 5

Paul Anka
ABC / MCA / Universal Music

The Bobbettes
Atlantic Records

Screamin' Jay Hawkins
Okeh Records / Sony Music

Chapter 6

Telegram from Herald Records
Larry Esposito

Dick Clark on American Bandstand
ABC TV archives / Getty Images

Justine Carelli and Bob Clayton
ABC TV archives

Sassafrass and Chapel on the Hill
Cash Box / Herald Records / Neil Arena

Chapter 7

George Lorenz
Buffalo Music Hall of Fame

Hound Dog Tour poster
Neil Arena

The Tune Weavers
Casa Grande / Ember / Herald

Jerry Lee Lewis
Sun Records; public domain

Chapter 8

Al Benson
WGES / Chancellor Media

Priscilla Bowman with Jay McShann
Jasmine Records

Big Maybelle
Flickr / confirmed as public domain

The Dells
Vee-Jay records / Queen Booking Corporation publicity

Chapter 9

Al Silver
Ellen Silver Stange

Herald's Hot in '57
Cash Box / Neil Arena

Wake County Courthouse
State Archives of North Carolina, Raleigh; public domain

Andy Wilson record review
Cash Box 1957

Andy Wilson record label
Athens Records, Nashville; public domain

Chapter 10

Huey Smith and his Clowns
Ace Records

Larry Williams
Speciality Records / London Records

Bo Diddley
Chess records; public domain

Chapter 11

Royal Theater, Baltimore
Maryland Center for History and Culture

The Del-Vikings, 1957
Fee Bee / Dot Records

Screamin' Jay Hawkins
ABC TV; public domain

Chapter 12

George Hamilton IV
Colonial records; ABC-Paramount

Frankie Avalon
Chancellor Records publicity; ABC-Paramount

Bobby Darin
General Artists Corporation; public domain

Chapter 13

Ardsley Country Club
Courtesy of the Westchester County Historical Society

Joni James
GAB Archives / Redferns

Mel Tillis
Columbia Records

Murray the K
Audacy, Inc

Legal letter
Neil Arena

Chapter 14

Everly Brothers tour poster
Neil Arena

Herald the Beat
Neil Arena

Most Valued Player
Neil Arena

Sassafrass flyer
Cash Box; Herald / Ember Records publicity

The Mello-Kings
Neil Arena

Neil and Valerie Jones
Jones Family Collection

Printed in Great Britain
by Amazon